INHALE · EXHALE · REPEAT

A meditation handbook
for every part of your day

Emma Mills

LONDON • SYDNEY • AUCKLAND • JOHANNESBURG

1 3 5 7 9 10 8 6 4 2

Rider, an imprint of Ebury Publishing,
20 Vauxhall Bridge Road,
London SW1V 2SA

First published in 2017 by Rider Books

Rider is part of the Penguin Random House group of companies whose
addresses can be found at global.penguinrandomhouse.com

www.penguinrandomhouse.co.uk

A CIP catalogue record for this book is available from the British Library

ISBN 9781846045295

MIX
Paper from
responsible sources
FSC
www.fsc.org
FSC® C018179

Printed and bound in Great Britain by Clays Ltd, St Ives PLC

Penguin Random House is committed to a sustainable future for
our business, our readers and our planet. This book is made
from Forest Stewardship Council® certified paper.

Important note: meditation is not a substitute for traditional healthcare
or therapy. If you are experiencing mental health problems, please consult
a qualified healthcare practitioner before undertaking a complementary
wellbeing programme such as this one. Before following the dietary advice
in this book, please consult a doctor or medical professional if
experiencing health problems in which diet might be a factor.

XB

Emma Mills is a writer and meditation teacher with a passion for sharing ideas about living well. She helped to pioneer a new form of poetry therapy with MIND and the NHS, and is the mindfulness expert on the board of advisers at Neom Organics. Today, she has her own private practices in London and the Midlands. Emma holds events across the UK, and frequently travels overseas to present workshops and collaborate with leading brands on special projects.

Also by Emma Mills:

Relish

CONTENTS

PART THREE: POST-WORK DETOX

PART FOUR: DAYS OFF

FOREWORD

I don't know about you, but I think life is precious.

I want to feel free and joyful all the time – not just during designated moments like the five minutes at the end of yoga or during the four-week holiday period.

Wouldn't it be great if we could find calm and happiness whatever we're doing – at work, in relationships, even if we're busy trying to change the world? Feeling this good could help us get it right more often with those we care for, and see us step into important meetings with nothing to prove and everything to give, feeling wholly comfortable in our own skin.

There is a new sort of calm and you don't have to be a saint to experience it. It involves a simple inner shift that turns every new day into an adventure.

One of the keys to this way of being is meditation, a simple practice that's available to you whoever you are. It's not about undertaking a personality transplant, it's just about tapping into that deep river of calm that we all have access to.

I am hugely passionate about helping you to feel happier and healthier through not only meditation, but a holistic approach to life that includes a balanced diet, wellbeing, good work, creativity and also beauty – whether for you that means MAC or *Macbeth*.

Life's too short for unnecessary suffering and a lack of loving connection between us, so wherever you are, at whatever stage of life, get to it!

I hope this book will be the travel guide you need to navigate the modern day with style and grace.

With love,
Emma

HOW TO USE
THIS BOOK

This twenty-four-hour guide draws inspiration from neuroscience, the arts and Eastern wisdom. Please dip in and out of these pages during the day to find a meditation to suit the moment. Alternatively read it from start to finish for a nice grounding in meditative life. I've based the comings and goings of this guide on the lives of many of the people I meet in the city. Please feel welcome to keep hold of the meditations that suit you best and apply them to your schedule.

Here are a few interesting ways to use this book:

1.   Turn to Part One first thing in the morning and pick an inspired meditation to start the day with.

2.   Prepare for a big work event using the simple focusing meditations in Part Two.

3.   Overwhelmed by 3 p.m.? Try the Gap Meditation on page 51 and re-start your afternoon with clarity and calm.

4.   If you often open a bottle of wine after a long day, try first flicking through to Part Three; take the Switch Off From Work Meditation and transition happily from day to night.

5.   You can discover and mindfully cook recipes for healthy meals in Part Four.

6.   Unlock the joy of days off by trying the Art and Beauty Meditations, also in Part Four.

7.   Open this book at the appropriate time of day and get back on the wellbeing wagon, feeling great once again, wherever you are!

TIP: Read the poem 'The Little Vagabond' by William Blake to stay cheerful and warm on your mindful path.

INTRODUCTION

Just like physical exercise, meditation can take many forms.

Focusing

Essentially, meditation is an activity that asks you to focus your attention in a particular way. This could be by concentrating on the sight of a flower, listening to a voice as it leads you through a guided meditation, or simply by focusing on your own breath as you inhale and exhale. Sometimes you'll do it with an aim in mind, such as improving your concentration or relaxing after a long day at work.

Enquiring

Meditation is also a chance to gather your thoughts and reflect on yourself and your life. From this quiet reflection you'll grow used to sitting in that inner space I call 'The Middle' (see page 9). From there, you can start to explore ideas about life or even make enquiries into the nature of things, such as, for example, deciding to meditate on what animates a flower or a topic like 'the nature of innovation', or perhaps contemplating the Pink Floyd album *The Dark Side of the Moon*.

Being

Some of the meditations in this guide invite you to focus your attention in one direction or another. Others have a goal or revolve around something you are looking into. Yet meditation can also be a time to sit quietly and just be – without any agenda. Here you have an opportunity to let thoughts, feelings and senses appear, unfold and dissolve. This 'just being' approach can give us some much needed breathing room.

Meditation key:

It's wise to meditate with an attitude of discovery. In doing so, you leave the door of opportunity wide open and the many wonderful, yet unexpected benefits of meditation will come your way. Each meditation in this book can offer you its own set of special qualities. Some promote focus and concentration, others have a nice calming effect, and the fun, explorative practices spark inspiration. The meditations here have been divided into three categories and you can use this key to find one to suit your mood in any given moment.

Meditations to inspire ⚡
Meditations for focus 👁
Meditations for calm 🪷

A (Very) Short History

Archaeologists agree that the origins of meditation are many thousands of years old, dating to about 5,000 to 3,500 BCE. It developed in Buddhist India, Taoist China, Persia and Japan before coming over to the West. However, meditation is essentially a lay practice and – just like swimming – its purpose changes in line with the intention of the meditator: for instance, a swimmer might want to cool down in a pool or cross the channel. Over the centuries, many teachers have had to ground their work in one religion or another in order to avoid being seen as heretics, but don't feel you have to become a Buddhist or Hindu or subscribe to a faith in order to meditate. We can make up our own rules and practise meditation exactly as we want to. Incorporate meditation's lessons into your own way of living and find out what is true for you.

Some Science

In recent years, there has been a lot of scientific research into mindfulness. This is a modern, secular strand of meditation that is often defined as cultivating a sense of moment-to-moment, non-judgemental awareness. It involves paying attention in a specified way to the present moment.

Many of the practices in this guide draw on mindfulness, because it is an approach that works well 'on the go' and alongside daily activities such as washing up or cooking a meal.

Research in neuroscience suggests that simple mindfulness practices can create real change in the brain, reducing anxiety and fear, and improving compassion, cognitive ability and creativity. For much of the twentieth century, it was thought that neuro-plasticity – the brain's ability to reinvent itself – was purely a feature of prenatal and early childhood development, but this is now understood to last in adulthood. This means, for example, that the brain can develop positive new programmes throughout adult life.

It is never too late to be happy.

The Poetry of Calm

In 1910, the founder of psychoanalysis, Sigmund Freud, said, 'Everywhere I go I find a poet has been there before me.' Never one to be late for the party, Freud recognised how frequently poets point to the essential parts of life that we all share. You know, the real grit and bones of being. These kinds of insight can be found in many styles of poetry throughout the ages, ranging from the writings of Rumi, Hafiz and Blake, to Emily Dickinson, D. H. Lawrence, P. B. Shelly, Rilke and Fernando Pessoa. These and other great writers often point to the great stillness of presence through their work. In this sense, poems are like little intravenous shots of meditation.

There are lots of literary tips shared throughout this book, so do give them a go. Don't worry if you're new to poems or feel unsure about them. It's as simple as 1, 2, 3:

1.   Read it
2.   How does it make you feel? Do you like it?
3.   If you like it, read it again; if you don't, move onto the next!

Bringing It All Together in the Digital Age

Meditation has played the perfect drag act in its 5,000-year passage from East to West. In every evolution it has taken on the perfume of its era, with various schools of thought all basically speaking about the same thing.

This, right now, is the digital information age, and meditation is being championed by a new generation of teachers. The issues we face are different to those of Rumi, Rilke and Buddha because the landscape of our lives has changed. But how?

While a hectic pace of life has been a matter of concern for some time now, the seemingly relentless innovation in information technology is quite new and poses a unique challenge to our generation. With meditation to hand, we can put our best foot forward and navigate the fast-changing demands of today with calm, focus and inspiration.

Getting Started!

Some key meditation terms.

At certain points during the course of this book we'll save time by speaking in code. So, when we say, 'Take an Easy Breath and adopt the Ready position', we will know instantly how to begin – without having to go through the rigmarole of remembering lengthy routines. Here are a few key guidelines:

Easy Breath

Resting gently where you are, notice the coming and going of your breath. In and out, in and out. No effort or intervention, just watching and listening keenly.

Easy Seat

1.   Sit on a high-backed chair, nice and upright, with your feet firmly planted on the ground, hands turned palm uppermost and resting in your lap.
2.   Sit cross-legged on the floor, again with your back feeling nice and perky but not uncomfortable. If you find crossed legs a bit of a stretch, it can help to pop a cushion or a rolled-up yoga mat under your sitting bones. This also helps keep your spine upright.

Mantras

Mantras are as simple as saying a few choice words aloud or inwardly, or voicing a particular sound such as humming. The sound in question is repeated several times, allowing it to sink in. Sound your mantras while sitting in an Easy Seat, or perhaps while standing upright with your hands hanging loosely at your sides. Whichever you choose, be sure to give yourself plenty of room to breathe so you can express yourself fully.

Being Ready

'Being Ready' feels almost as though you are expecting something, but not anything in particular – just ready to be happy, ready to meet whatever shows up in life. To Be Ready first relax your shoulders and take an easy breath or two. Have your mind and body slip into neutral. You're at rest, yet fully attentive and listening to life. I imagine this is how cats rest— relaxed but still alert.

The Middle

Sit firmly in the middle of your being the way a hinge sits in a door. Life and experiences are unfolding around you, and yet you remain the quiet knower of all these comings and goings without getting caught up in them.

Sometimes things happen and you will get drawn in by distractions – and move away from The Middle. One of the tell-tale signs that you have moved out of The Middle is a feeling of discontentment, or not feeling quite yourself. But don't worry! Often just recognising this is enough to trigger our natural return to The Middle.

You could consider the game of tennis as a nice analogy here. The tennis player is encouraged to return to the middle of the base line between each shot. From the middle they are in the best position possible from which to return the next shot – which could be heading to any part of the court. Eventually, you might find that even though you are returning shots left, right and centre, the feeling of being in 'The Middle' comes with you wherever you go.

Breathing Exercises

There are several different breathing exercises in this guide, each inviting you to explore your breath in various ways. It is important to go gently here. If it doesn't feel good, stop doing it. Never force or strain your breath or do anything that makes you uncomfortable. Likewise, if you have a pre-existing health condition, be sure to consider the guidance of your healthcare professional beforehand.

Accessories

Basics

- A pillow, comfortable cushion or chair to sit in.
- A designated safe place identified as a good spot for your meditation.
- A journal and pen.

Extras

- Your favourite music playlist, plus headphones.
- Herbal teas (chamomile, peppermint, jasmine, for example).
- Poetry anthology and a book of short stories (see recommendations in this book).
- Home-grown herbs for herbal tea and pot plants for creating relaxing surroundings.
- Plenty of organic fruit and veg for the recipes in the book.
- Essential oils and aromatherapy fragrances to spritz (lavender, jasmine, rosewood, for example).
- Soft and comfortable clothes for sitting in.

Ok, let's get started!

STARTING THE DAY

UPON RISING: take a few moments to relish your freshly woken moment.

EARLY MORNING: enjoy five to ten minutes of meditation with a hot lemon tea. Finish with a little light stretching or movements.

BREAKFAST: savour a bowl of seedy oats in the summer, or warm up with a healing soup in the autumn.

GETTING READY: follow breakfast with a shower, taking your time to notice each part of your body as you lather up with some beautiful essential oils and natural soaps. Dress with joy and cultivate the attitude of expecting to encounter something great in your day.

SELF-REFLECTION: before you set out for the day, read a poem or an inspired quote from your journal.

STEPPING OUT: consider your intentions for the day – the things that are important to you and those you love – and step out with an attitude of embracing them.

TIP: Spend a little time outdoors first thing in the morning. The trend for Forest Bathing, which, put simply, means spending time in nature for the benefit of your health, is on the rise thanks to the growing research supporting the healing properties of the natural world. (We'll explore the beauty of nature in Part Four.)

WAKING

My eyes open and it feels like I'm immediately caught up in thoughts of everything I need to do with my morning before I head to work. Yet in those precious few moments, between waking up and regaining full consciousness, there is a little sparkle of serenity. Sometimes it's bright and at other times it passes almost imperceptibly as the mind kicks in with a barrage of thoughts.

Spotting this freshly-woken moment is special, because it offers you the opportunity to catch your life turning itself back on, and allows you to watch the machine of your mind slowly cranking up though the gears. This is the moment that Harold Monro describes in his poem 'Living':

> And in a moment Habit, like a crane,
> Will bow its neck and dip its pulleyed cable,
> Gathering me, my body, and our garment,
> And swing me forth, oblivious of my question,
> Into the daylight – why?

This is where we'll start our mindful day. The very moment you open your eyes.

Meditation: (Very) Early Morning

(5 minutes) *

Here's how to get started:

1. Spot the moment the outside world comes into view and you, in all your glory, reappear in the story of life.
2. When you spot it, simply lay quietly in your bed.
3. Notice the innocent freshness in those first few moments.
4. Don't be concerned with grasping or prolonging the moment, just notice it while it's there.
5. What are some of the first things you become aware of?
6. Could it be the feel of the sheets, the temperature of the room, your thoughts and ideas, the weight of your body in bed and the beat of your heart? Let it all happen.
7. You could imagine becoming porous and soaking up the moment like one of those luxury spa sponges – entirely intimate and in touch with life.

By starting out in a gently attentive fashion you'll set yourself up nicely to notice your life as it unfolds, in big and small ways, throughout your day.

* These are suggested timings, but please feel free to adapt them to your routine.

Waking Up Bright Eyed and Bushy Tailed

(5 minutes)

In the early hours of the morning your brain will start working hard to prepare you for your wake-up. The brain is very receptive at this time of day and whatever activity happens in those early moments is priceless.

Once you are awake, start as you mean to go on by focusing on something inspiring. For instance, swap your newspaper for your journal and enjoy a few moments of self-reflection. Alternatively, spend ten minutes leafing through a photo book or a beautiful catalogue.

Planning Your Morning Routine in Advance . . .

(15 minutes after waking)

I don't know how similar we are, you and I, but sometimes it's – I don't know – Tuesday night, say, and I think, 'Yes, tomorrow I will get up early, maybe 5 a.m. Hell, let's make it 4.30. And I'll run four miles in the park before work. I'll make juices and smoothies and do this, that and the other.'

Then, I actually wake up in the morning and the 'me' who wakes up isn't interested at all; she just wants to press Snooze and sleep in. Why does this happen?

The Russian philosopher Gurdjieff suggests that most people lack a unified consciousness and are prey to the fluctuations of their minds. In this way, many 'I's arise and dissolve each moment.

There may be an 'I' who says one morning, 'No, you don't need to go for that swim, you're tired. Just have a lie in and enjoy tea and croissants instead – why not, you're in charge!' And there is another I that surfaces, post tea and croissant, to say, 'Oh, you're terrible, look what you've done!' Are these all the same I? Who knows, but there are a couple of things you can do to take control of your morning:

- Put your clean gym clothes or a pillow for meditation next to your bed so that when you wake up they are there, ready and waiting.
- Prepare a healthy lunch in the evening to take to work the next day. (This is likely to prevent the 'I' that couldn't give two hoots about your nutritious living plan when it's 4 p.m. and you're starving and the only thing left at Prêt is a cheese baguette).

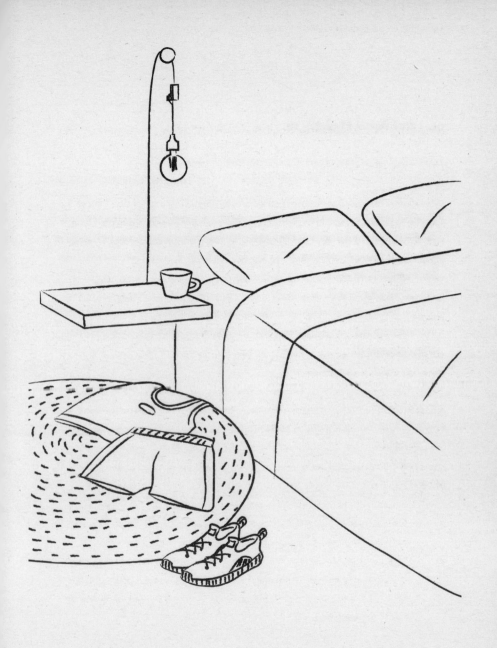

... But Don't Overdo It!

'You cannot waste tomorrow; it is kept for you.'

Arnold Bennett (1867–1931)

Planning ahead is not about becoming neurotic; it's simply about getting to know ourselves well, including our little ways. All the same, excess planning doesn't leave much room for spontaneity. For joy. For aliveness. It is important to remember that freedom is fabulous.

So what to do?

There might be meetings to get to and responsibilities to share, but allow yourself to be open to plans changing. Why not let yourself have your morning, when it happens?

Meditation: Checking Your Diary

(10 minutes)

- Take an Easy Seat and a few Easy Breaths.
- Close your eyes and begin to imagine your perfect day in all its glory.
- Take your time over the special details that will make all the difference.

Raise your visualisation to the next level by adding emotion. Immerse yourself now in the feelings you would be having during your dream day. This way you don't wait for your perfect day to actually happen before you start feeling amazing.

TIP: In doing this meditation you'll highlight any ideas you currently have about what's possible for you. For example, the chances are that your imaginary day will involve activities that you currently conceive of as viable or that are likely to be based on past experience. This meditation is a good reminder that while visualisation is a great tool, it is often reliant on the mind and the mind itself might be limited in terms of what it's able to conceive.

Waking Up on the Wrong Side of Bed

Despite all your positive bedtime preparation (see Part Three), sometimes you might wake up feeling blue.

Perhaps you are stressed and overwhelmed at work, and the thought of getting up and going at it again is almost too much. Maybe there are some concerns in your personal life. You might even wake up blue for no apparent reason, which seems most unfair!

More often than not, it isn't necessarily the blue mood that causes suffering but our thoughts about it – our abstraction. The mere presence of our blue mood freaks us out and then we spend a lot of time thinking about why it's there and how to get rid of it – and this freaks us out further. Then we notice we are freaking out and that freaks us out further still. Ad infinitum.

An Alternative Approach

The mind goes through a charade of over-processing our feelings because it really likes to know what's going on (especially when it's not happy about something and wants to get rid of that something ASAP). This defensive style of thinking gives the mind a sense of agency; it feels like it's on top of the job – and who doesn't like being on top of the job, right?

In time, and with a little self-awareness, we can get wise to the mind's tendencies and find ourselves better equipped not to get sucked into that mental loop again. Instead we can entertain the possibility that:

> This morning you woke up like this. It's allowed. It's no more personal than waking up to a sky full of sun or rain. Trust that if you get up and put one foot in front of the other, it will soon pass – everything does.

TIP: Try not to fear or fight feelings. On the contrary, welcome them and accept them. As soon as you do, they will be neutralised.

Meditation: Simple Morning Breath Counting

(5 minutes max.)

Breath counting is a good and simple way to calm both the nervous system and the overworked mind. When your exhale is even a few counts longer than your inhale, the vagus nerve, which runs from the neck down through the diaphragm, sends a signal to your brain to turn up your parasympathetic nervous system (the rest-and-relax system) and turn down your sympathetic nervous system (the stress response). With counted breathing, we aim to balance the in- and out-breath so that the out-breath is just a touch longer than the in-breath, or at least equal to it.

- Take an Easy Seat, and begin following some Easy Breaths for two to three minutes. Try to breathe using your nose for this exercise, if it feels comfortable.
- Begin to count the length of both your in-breath and out-breath. You can do this aloud or just quietly in your mind. Is the in-breath longer than the out-breath? Or vice versa? See what happens if, with very little effort (you don't want to push hard now), you bring the in- and out-breath into balance, so they are equal in length. This gives you a chance to regulate the flow of oxygen around the body.

Meditation: Energising Morning Moves

(5 minutes)

This is a fantastic movement sequence that encourages us to feel part of life, getting us ready to share our voice with the world. Try these moves standing upright, with your arms at your sides. Right, let's get started!

1. Gently sweep your right hand out at thigh height over the ground as though you are sowing seeds, turning your body from left to right moving the outstretched arm in an arc. Gently repeat this sowing motion from right to left with your left arm outstretched.

2. Next, standing upright again, with both arms at your sides, bend to the right and look down at your right hand, then bring it in an arc-shape up and round, over the top of your head. Reach it as far over to the left as you can while watching it. When you are leaning over to the left as far as you can comfortably stretch, let the right arm just swing back round. Now do the same with your left arm, leaning over to the right.

3. Stand back straight and look out at the horizon, raising your left arm up straight in front of you and moving it all the way round the left, following your hand with your face as your turn – all the time surveying the morning horizon. Do the same with the right hand.

4.   Now imagine walking up a mountain: start by marching on the spot with your knees raised high for a few moments.

5.   Having marched to the top, stand still and bring both arms up and out in front of you before letting them open out to your sides. Then place your hands, palms down, on your lower back. Lean back ever so slightly and open up your chest, out to the world.

6.   Drop your hands back to your sides and make both your hands into loose fists. Then, using your knuckles, begin to tap gently around your chest and the front and back of your ribcage. Let out a little 'ahhh ... ' sound as you tap, before letting your hands fall to your sides again.

7.   Last but not least, let's use the voice you'll take out into the world. Start by making the lowest note you can possibly make on your next out-breath – perhaps it's a deep 'huur' sound. Then, on your next out-breath, make a sound that's in between your highest and lowest sound. Finally, on your next exhale make the highest pitched sound you can. Stamp your feet several times confidently on the spot to ground yourself. Now you are ready and (hopefully) keen to take your place in the world!

TIP: Go gently and move at the pace that suits you best. When performed mindfully, your stretches can become part of your morning meditation.

BREAKFAST

Some people quite like routine, perhaps getting up at 5 a.m. every day to run, meditate, do yoga and breakfast like a king – and finding solace in this kind of rhythm. Where there is rhythm, there is life. However, others might recoil in horror at the thought of monotony and ritual, and prefer just to see what happens at the start of each new day. It's good to follow your own inclinations here, but whatever your preference, one thing to ensure you don't miss out on is breakfast.

Here are my top breakfast tips:

- Settle into your day gently. You aren't a workhorse so be good to yourself.
- Wherever possible make time each morning for some self-reflection exercises or health and wellness treats. Far better to set off into the next part of your day with your best foot forward.
- A wise teacher once told me the key to a long happy life was to do it differently on Sunday. Different cereal, magazines and a walk. Perhaps he was onto something .... (See Part Four for some suggestions.)

Simple, Healthy Breakfasts

Oats and Wild Seeds

Serves 1

1 small cup organic rolled oats
1 tbsp raw nuts: walnuts, almonds, cashews or Brazil nuts
1 tsp raw seeds: chia seeds, linseeds, sunflower seeds or pumpkin seeds
Milk or nut milk to serve

Method: mix together the ingredients in your favourite breakfast bowl.

This breakfast can work especially well if you have an early start and not much time! As you can choose which combination of nuts and seeds you prefer, it's also a good reminder of the way we can create our own perfect meditation practice. A sprinkle of this, a handful of that, a dash of the other.

From Russia with Love: Healthy Breakfast Soup

Serves 4

2 tbsp extra-virgin olive oil
3 shallots
4 organic small to medium-sized beetroots, with the leaves on
1 stick celery
1 green bell pepper
1 bunch of radishes
1 small bunch of rainbow chard
½ tsp Himalayan pink salt
Freshly-ground black pepper (to taste)
½ lemon
1 tbsp freshly-chopped parsley, to garnish

Method: heat the olive oil in a large pan. Chop and add the vegetables to the pan, leaving aside a few radishes. Cover the vegetables with boiling water and heat until the beetroot begins to turn soft. Allow to cool and then blend into a thick soup. Water down the mixture to your taste before serving. Divide into four portions and serve with lots of freshly-ground black pepper, a squeeze of lemon juice and garnished with a sprinkling of chopped parsley and a few radishes on the side.

TIP: The short story 'Gooseberries' by Anton Chekhov is a great accompaniment to this healthy, grounding soup.

Keep a Quote Book

It's important to read something motivating each morning. The text doesn't have to be spiritual, but certainly reading something that is inspiring to you – maybe in the form of a short piece of prose or a heart-warming quote – can help you to start the day firmly in The Middle.

Keep a quote book specifically for the beautiful insights you've garnered and the many things in life there are to be grateful for. Then you can dip into it before you start the day.

Why is this helpful? Our conditioning – the way we have been brought up to see the world – is often heavy and multi-generational, so it's good to keep reminding ourselves of those uplifting things we once read about and resonated with.

TIP: Leave a little digital gap for yourself by keeping your devices switched off until you decide you are ready to communicate with the outside world.

7 Poems to Inspire Your Quote Book

The list below is a beautiful collection of poems, one for each day of the week. My favourite line at the moment is from 'Victoria Market' by Francis Brabazon. It's the bit about the sun coming up between the rows of vegetables, which reminds me that wonderful changes can happen little by little.

1.   'Begin' by Brendan Kennelly (b.1936)
2.   'Apple Blossom' by Louis MacNeice (1907–1963)
3.   'Days' by Philip Larkin (1922–1985)
4.   'Wow' by Hafiz (c.1326–1389)
5.   'It Ain't What You Do, It's What It Does To You' by Simon Armitage (b.1963)
6.   'The Road Not Taken' by Robert Frost (1874–1963)
7.   'Victoria Market' by Francis Brabazon (1907–1984)

GETTING READY

Ok, you're up and awake! You've enjoyed a little early morning meditation, a spot of breakfast and perhaps even dipped into your quote book for a bit of inspiration. Now it's time to get washed and dressed with care and attention.

Although you might be pressed for time, it's best to avoid rushing: if you can stay calm and unflustered, you'll start the day firmly in 'The Middle' and feeling fully able to make the most of whatever the next few hours might bring.

Meditation: Showering

Apparently designer Tom Ford takes four baths a day, and two of those are before 9.15 a.m. That man is living his life.

Option One

(20 minutes)

Step into the shower as though you were stepping off the plane onto foreign terrain.

- Savour the different sensations and aromas available in the moment.
- Shower with thoughtfulness. It can be an incredibly meditative time of day, full of fruitful insights and ideas, so be sure to stay alert and Ready.

Option Two

(5 minutes)

You might be in a rush and you might be busy, but if you've decided to shower you may as well go with it. Pay full attention, take some Easy Breaths and immerse yourself in the experience even if it's just for a few minutes.

Taking Action and Letting Go

You've geared yourself up physically and mentally, and now you're ready to step out of the door and greet the day. However, some things remain out of our control – the weather, the commute, our family and colleagues.

Expectations always involve a projection of our thoughts and hopes onto the future, and can foster inflexible relations with the moment, followed by disappointment if things don't go our way. Whereas if you head off into your day with an attitude of embracing everything you encounter, you'll be better placed to respond to each situation uniquely as it arises.

A regular meditation practice helps us to make this embrace more easily. It helps us to go out of that front door with tenacity and a loving spirit – knowing full well that it's like setting out on an adventure without a map. This sort of welcoming attitude is true liberation and can be a perfect tonic to frustration and stress. After all, who's to say our way was right, anyway?

Approaching each moment with presence, or 'Being Ready' as I call it, will spark your ability to be truly inventive with the scenarios you encounter. You'll solve problems, feel courageous, and your spontaneity, sense of fun and bold nature will come out and shine.

AT WORK

WALKING TO WORK: nothing is old hat. Keep your eyes and ears peeled on your daily walk – inspiration can appear anywhere.

COMMUTING: pause for three Easy Breaths before you take the escalator, lift or stairs.

ON ARRIVAL: create a calming space to support a great day's work.

BE CREATIVE: take a sixty-second Gap Meditation between finishing one task and taking your next inspired action (see page 51). Clear direction for your best work often comes in unguarded moments.

ELEVENSES: make a herbal tea, step outside into the fresh air and read a poem from your anthology.

MEETINGS: savour the experience of working with others towards a shared goal. If you need a pick-me-up, take a moment to check your posture and practise a few gentle stretches.

TIP: Giving all of yourself to your work means that whatever it is you are creating, be it a cup of coffee, a spreadsheet or an advertising campaign your work becomes the highest expression of your care and capabilities in any given moment.

THE COMMUTE

Believe it or not, your familiarity with your journey to work can make your commute fertile soil for cultivating presence. Here's how.

When the mind is familiar with a journey, it can switch on to autopilot and cruise along, paying less attention to its surroundings. That's because it perceives the route as a known and registered reality, therefore devoid of fresh interest. (This can also happen in our romantic relationships.) In this scenario, we come to rely increasingly on our memory rather than an awareness of what's occurring in the present moment.

No matter how many times you have made the journey to work, always be listening and looking. Wonder and loveliness can appear in unexpected places.

TIP: Say you're hell-bent on getting to that life-changing meeting (focusing on the destination rather than the journey, which is known in the meditation game as 'end gaining'), you risk missing the life-changing conversation the lady at the coffee house was trying to have with you as you rushed off.

Meditation: Walk to Work

(30 minutes, or length of your commute)

- Head out the door willing to see the world with fresh eyes.
- Feel your feet on the ground. Hear the sound of your footsteps – all that noise you are making. Your walking is part of this grand moment too.
- See if you can use your commute as an opportunity to be present. For example, pay attention to what's happening now, for the entirety of your commute. This way, each commute becomes a wonderful practice in present-moment awareness, as opposed to thirty minutes of random mental activity.
- Last but not least, be aware of this wonderful capacity you have: to be aware, awake and a part of this great life we share.

Feeling Overwhelmed by Commuters

'We are all here on earth to help others; what on earth the others are here for I don't know.'

John Foster Hall, comedian

Sometimes you're travelling to work and everything would be great – except for all those other people in your space. Here are some handy tricks for staying sane on the train.

Meditation: For the Thrill Seeker: The Wild West

The Indian mystic Swami Vivekenanda is said to have suggested that the best jobs for a truth seeker were in the armed forces or the police. I expect his reasoning was that these jobs require a person to navigate many a sticky situation.

I think the same can apply to the commute.

When intense situations arise, treat them like a rich, deeply vital yoga class. Get immersed in the entire experience.

- Approach the diversity of the commute like riding a raucous Wild West Train.
- Embrace the mass of life joining you for the trip.
- Don't resist the ruckus or cut yourself off from it with your book or your phone, for example. Instead move more deeply into the experience so that you can feel entirely intimate with life.

TIP: Read the poem 'Snow' by Louis MacNeice and laugh at how intense the world is sometimes.

Meditation: For the Intellectual: the Transparency

You feel overwhelmed by people being so close to you. You wish you could wrap yourself in a magical bubble to protect yourself against their thoughts, feelings and smells ...

Maybe some people are rude or smelly or dawdling. Watch carefully as their actions draw reactions from you – despite the fact that moments ago you were so chilled out. Before you know it, you too are drawn in and start to take your surroundings personally.

- Don't withdraw and don't aggress. Just remain in stillness, as though you have become transparent.
- Allow noises, smells and sly manoeuvres to pass through you, unable to get any purchase on you.
- Let it all happen. And remain the quiet observer of your reactions.
- Having nothing to grip on to and nothing to play the game with, life will start to hook into you less and feel easier.

Meditation: Improving Focus on the Train

(2 minutes)

Try choosing to keep your attention focused on the image or idea of an apple, or maybe the feeling of breathing in and out. See if you can keep your attention tied to your object of choice for the time spent between stops on the train. This works best if the time between stops is a couple of minutes long.

Meditation: Pause Points

(15 seconds)

Many mini meditations make for a very happy day. Pause for three conscious breaths before you take the lift, stars or elevator on your way to work.

AT THE OFFICE

When I say 'at the office', I really mean wherever you spend your day – at a desk, behind a counter, in a class room or on a ward. Wherever and however you make a living, there are plenty of ways to create great opportunities for yourself by being open to new ways of working.

One way to start is by taking a close look at your thoughts and your working habits. This will help you to spot areas ripe for innovation. Try to also open your arms to new ways of thinking and new people. Perhaps there is someone you know who goes about life in a different way to you – what can you learn from them by simply listening to them or watching the way that they work?

TIP: Read the poem 'The Vintage Man' by Hafiz.

Create an Inspired Workspace

(5 minutes)

For a Day at Your Desk

You'll need:

- A tea pot with herbal teas aplenty. Try fresh chocolate mint for focus and chamomile flowers for calm.
- A note book for ideas so you can stay on task while retaining your wonderful ideas.
- A small poetry anthology to dip into for a new perspective.
- A beautiful indoor plant to accompany you at your desk. Lemon balm has a great scent and works well in full shade or sunlight.
- A healthy lunchbox.
- Cosy socks you can pop on for those moments when you want to meditate at your desk. Having special socks for the occasion can help bring that 'at home' feeling to the office.
- A natural room fragrance to help your workspace smell like an aromatherapy haven.

TIP: As you spritz your room fragrance around your desk, and perhaps beyond, set the intention that you have for the day. For example, it might be: 'Today, I'm creating a space for creativity, focus and collaboration.'

For A Day Working On the Go

You'll need:

- To be organised. Arrange your day bag, making sure you have all the things you need, while clearing out unnecessary clutter and papers.
- A small bottle of essential oil. Try lavender for relaxation and eucalyptus for energy and focus.
- A note book for the inspiration you'll find on your travels.
- A healthy packed lunch and a small container with green juice powder in it, ready to dilute with water and drink for a healthy, energising pick-me-up.
- Headphones for listening to guided meditations or playlist music.

Meditation: Finding a Solution

(A few moments)

Sometimes when we need a solution we can try as we might to use our rational mind to solve the problem, but with no luck. Then perhaps we are out shopping one afternoon, minding our own business, and – bam! – the solution appears in an instant. Which is how a lot of understanding occurs. Do plenty of shopping!

Only joking ... Just let yourself be in the moment and see what arises. Or try a completely fresh approach, and a different activity, such as painting or dancing.

Listen to what comes into you in unguarded moments and then if necessary acquire the skills to bring those insights into fruition. The more you fulfil these impersonal wishes the better you will get at bringing them into fruition and the more readily they will appear. The cup of creativity is one that magically refills itself and never runs out.

The 'Gap' Meditation Set

The 'Gap' is what I like to refer to as the crack in the wall where the light can get in.

Leave lots of little empty spaces in your work. Space abhors a vacuum and wonderful things will emerge out of that wide, spacious gap. For example, when you are preparing a work presentation you make sure you learn all the facts and figures, and perhaps even practise beforehand; however, leaving a Gap means leaving room within the delivery of the presentation for spontaneity and for sudden inspiration to appear and keep your work fresh and of the moment.

The Gap Meditation

(5 minutes)

Keeping what we've learned about the Gap in mind, let's try a little something together. It takes just five minutes and it's perfect for those moments where we might find ourselves feeling confused, or at a loss for what to do next ...

- There is usually a brief gap between one task coming to completion and a new task starting up. See if you can spot this tiny pause and stay with it for a moment.
- Close your eyes and spend a moment exploring what it is like to be in this state of needlessness.
- Where do you feel this phenomenon in your body?
- When a new motivation or need arises, you'll become aware of the next task you wish to complete. Notice where this begins in the body. Does this new impetus have an accompanying sensation?
- Take a moment to consider the moment and marshal your troops. Then take informed action, embarking on the next task – whatever that may be for you.

Nothing is Missing

Practising the Gap meditation can remind us of how much we stand to gain from those moments of stillness: we can use them to replenish our energy, inspire our creativity and provide ourselves with a great platform from which to pick the best course of action to take next.

By noticing this pause, or Gap, you will become familiar with recognising what it feels like to *just be*, without any momentum.

The task that has just been completed has addressed the old need, and a new need has yet to appear in your mind to demand your attention. In those few blissful moments, you are content and nothing is missing. Ah ... heaven!

Things that Make Gaps More Likely

- Regular meditation.
- Making flexible plans and being spontaneous.
- Practising stream-of-consciousness writing.
- Exploring the arts of spoken word poetry, improv theatre and street art. Anything that makes you more familiar with the spirit of spontaneity.

Make Things with Love

It's really wonderful to see how pausing to be present can make such a big difference to your subsequent actions. Fully attentive, you're now in a great place to make things from this place of calm.

Things carry the vibe of their maker. That includes kisses, emails, hot dinners, websites and dresses.

Do things with love and enjoy the process. Do your best and do it for its own sake. Then, if your project isn't as well received as you'd have liked, you can still say that you enjoyed making it.

Have Confidence in Your Work

The fear surrounding creative works often comes from taking personal ownership of the things that are created. Making it all about you ...

If you want to be the best dancer, the best joiner, the best public speaker or fashion PR guru, then remove yourself from the equation and give all your love and attention to delivering the best work possible for the benefit of the whole.

Meditation: Elevenses

(10 minutes)

1. Make a mid-morning cup of fresh herbal tea and nip outside. Take a poetry anthology or your journal with you.
2. Take an Easy Seat and follow your Easy Breath for a few minutes. Try breathing through your nose for this activity.
3. Divide your next out-breath into four sections so that it comes out as four little pumps.
4. Do the same with the next in-breath, splitting the inhale into four equal sections like gasps.
5. Take this breathing pattern for six breaths so long as it feels good and comfortable.
6. It can sometimes help you to focus if you pop a hand over your stomach as you do this.
7. Let your breathing return to a very natural and normal pace.
8. Pick a poem at random from your anthology or journal to savour. You'll come back to your desk inspired with a refreshed perspective.

TIP: Read 'The Door', a beautiful poem by Miroslav Holub.

Meeting Remarkable People

Roles are useful because they shape the boundaries for our interactions with others – but they aren't the be-all and end-all. Becoming aware of our tacit assumptions around roles and hierarchies at work can help liberate us from any old patterns that shape our feelings and relationships with others.

Quite often we interface with our mental concepts of each other, rather than with the real deal. It's not surprising that so many miscommunications arise.

You could imagine that our mental concepts form a kind of plastic ball around us. The plastic ball in this analogy reminds me of the 90s TV show *The Gladiators*. In the show, competitors had to navigate an obstacle course while rolling around inside their giant plastic gladiator ball. There would never be any actual contact between two gladiators, because as soon as they were close enough to one another their balls would collide.

Meditation: The Gladiator

(5 minutes)

- Approach your co-worker at the water cooler.
- Notice the mental labels you have dressed that person up in: rich, skinny, healthy, French, rude, clever, etc.
- Some of those layers of perception may be contributing to your feelings of fear, enjoyment or discomfort in your co-worker's company.
- Peel away these ideas one by one until you see your co-worker purely and simply as he or she appears now. (For further guidance on this, use my Undressed Banana Meditation in Part Three.)

Your co-worker is just another person like you and perhaps you have more in common than you first thought. Now you've seen behind the curtain, so to speak. You know who your colleague really is and you can relax and enjoy a natural interaction with them without fear or intimidation.

Conflict Resolution

'There are a great many opinions in this world, and a good half of them are professed by people who have never been in trouble.'

Anton Chekhov (1860–1904), 'A Misfortune'

We may all have done things that were a bit rude. Been late for meetings, upset our colleagues and broken the trust of people we care about.

We're likely to attribute our own *faux pas* to the circumstances surrounding our misdeeds. Whereas, with other people, we are more likely to make assumptions and attribute it to a deadly flaw in their character: 'Look at him driving so fast, the lunatic!'

A cornerstone of the mindful pathway is non-judgement. We tend to be less judgemental when we understand the circumstances that surround someone's behaviour. Now, that isn't to say that we aren't discerning or that we condone unthoughtful behaviour, but it helps to appreciate that people don't do things in a vacuum. Their choices are influenced by a whole culture, including society, the cosmos, their lineage, what they had for breakfast and what was on TV that morning.

What's more, with every puddle we ourselves step into, we are likely to become less and less judgemental of those who have done the same. We become gentler with ourselves and gentler with the world.

Reaching a Resolution: Go For the Third Way

(5 to 10 minutes)

One way of navigating conflict at work is to put aside, just for a moment, any ideas we may have about who is right and who is wrong. With these to one side, we can work towards developing a nonbiased understanding of the situation.

- Start by examining your own viewpoint and the case you are putting forward.
- Then, in any way that seems appropriate, put yourself in the other person's shoes, as though you were going to defend their side of the story. Arguing the other person's side can take a bit of getting used to, especially if you are quite fixed in your own position. But do persevere, it's well worth it!
- Next consider the impersonal third-person perspective. I like to think of that perspective as a really wise old grandparent who sees all sides of the story as though from above, who understands fully, doesn't take sides and who offers objective, loving guidance to all involved. This grandparent doesn't have a personal agenda so it's easier for them to see the situation as a whole and how it might be resolved in a way that is in line with the greater good – as opposed to the personal good i.e.: what *I* want to have happened.
- Try to see the bigger picture of what has taken place and imagine how that wise grandparent might advise you.

After seeing things from all three perspectives, you might still fail to agree on things, but, in prioritising understanding over proving who is right or wrong, you could gain a fresh and balanced appreciation of the situation, which hopefully means it won't happen again.

TIP: There may even be another perspective from which to view the situation ... can you think of one?

Meditation and Mindful Movements: The Chess Board

(5 minutes)

Try this movement sequence to cultivate a sense of energy, confidence and presence. Start by standing up straight, with your arms by your sides, your eyes open and relaxed.

1. Tense the feet, and then tense the legs, the thighs, buttocks, and tense the stomach and shoulders, the neck and head. Now release the head, the neck, the shoulders, the chest, and work right down through the body, through the hips, the buttocks, the thighs, the shins and the feet; letting go of all and any tension.

2. On your next exhale, bring your hands up to your chest area and then take your arms straight out in front of you, palms uppermost as if you are making an offering or giving something away. Then sweep them out to the sides and back up to your heart again. (This looks a little like doing the breaststroke while swimming.) As you breathe out, give away the weight of the day; on each exhale, give it back to life to be washed, cleansed and otherwise carried away. After three or four outward motions, let your arms come to your sides and rest for a moment. How does it feel, now you are free of that weight?

3.   Perform the opposite motion with your arms, over the course of the next four in-breaths. Take the arms out to the sides at right angles to your body and sweep them out in front of you, before bringing them inwards towards you. It's almost as though you're welcoming someone in for a hug. As you inhale, imagine that you are taking in all the nourishment, ideas, and inspiration around you. After three or four inward motions let your arms come to your sides. Feel yourself charged, tall and standing and strong.

4.   With your feet hip-width apart, take a little jump to the right, making a firm stomp as you plant your feet on the ground. As you plant them, affirm, 'I am here, and I'm ready.' Now jump back to where you were, and from here affirm, 'Now I'm here, and I'm ready.' Then you might choose to jump forward or backward, left or right, like the Queen on a chess board. Take your time with each move you make, and feel yourself as being grounded and Ready from any position.

TIP: Remember to go steady and gentle, always breathing at your own pace. If you prefer, you can sit in a comfortable, high-backed chair for this sequence.

LUNCH

Lunch can be a moment of liberation in the working day. So much more than just another hour spent rushing around fulfilling chores, it offers us the chance to reset our inner compass, learn something new and nourish ourselves with good, healthy food. It's also a great opportunity to escape from your desk or workplace if you can, and get a breath of fresh air or do a bit of exercise. By stepping away from your desk, you'll re-energise yourself and return to your work feeling refreshed – rather than just sitting there, chewing a sandwich in front of your computer screen and sensing your energy levels plummet as you plough on into the afternoon. And why not make the most of this window in the day to socialise with your colleagues too?

TIP: Plants can bring a welcome boost to wellbeing and productivity. Lemon balm, cacti and Peperomia (radiator) plants work particularly well indoors. Take a moment after lunch to water the plants near you with care and attention, nurturing them as well as yourself.

Lunch Meditation: Get Lost

(10 minutes to 1 hour, depending on how lost you get)

Go for an aimless walk and see where you end up. As you walk, pay attention to your surroundings: what do you see, who do you meet?

On one or two exceptional occasions, I've found myself lost somewhere just outside the Bank of England while doing this – a long way from where I set out. So do take a map or your phone if you have to be back on time. If you can't get outdoors, maybe you can wander round the building; you never know what you'll find.

Mediterranean Lunch Bowl

Give yourself a lift in the middle of the day! This recipe is made with mostly raw vegetables. I like to think of it as the lunchbox equivalent of *The Grapes of Paradise* by the British writer H. E. Bates. Set among luscious Italian lakes and rolling Mediterranean hillsides, his romantic novellas bring a welcome – and ever so slightly scandalous – warmth to the afternoon!

Serves 2

1 handful mixed salad leaves, washed and finely chopped
½ cucumber, chopped into small pieces
1 avocado, sliced
2 heaped tbsp of mixed seeds (pumpkin, sesame, chia, for example)
5 cherry tomatoes, chopped into quarters
4 sundried tomatoes, chopped
½ red onion, chopped into long thin slices
1 handful flat-leaf parsley, finely chopped
1 handful chickpeas, precooked
4 sprigs purple sprouting broccoli, washed and chopped into florets
8 black olives
1 tbsp oil (e.g. extra-virgin olive oil, hemp oil, cold-pressed avocado oil)
½ lemon

Method: add all the chopped ingredients to your salad bowl and season with black pepper, your choice of oil and a good squeeze of the juice of half a lemon. Bon appétit!

TIP: If salad leaves alone won't keep your home fires burning till tea time, add a handful of noodles to this dish. There are quite a few alternatives to traditional egg, wheat or rice noodles available, such as edamame bean noodles or kelp noodles for example.

Reading Aloud At Lunchtime

(20 to 60 minutes, depending on how long you have)

Many of the conversations we have with our colleagues relate to our work, with a few friendly interludes in which we share our weekend news or discuss last night's dinner, perhaps. At times it can be hard to know what to talk about with people at work.

One way to introduce fun and enlightening conversations into your workplace is to read something brief and interesting together with your co-workers, and then chat about it. Having the text as your shared focus dispels the awkwardness of having to conjure conversation out of thin air. It can invite fresh exchanges on really fun topics, help you share and learn cool things about one another, and widen your perspective for the afternoon. Perfect!

How to get started:

- Pick a short story or poem that you feel enthusiastic about. And, if possible, something that others will also enjoy and relate to.
- Make a pot of herbal tea to share. Fresh peppermint, cardamom or fennel teas can be quite refreshing after lunch!
- Give everyone a copy of the material and take turns to read aloud with the other people listening and following along.
- Do it with a sense of light heartedness and discovery – and with little concern for outcomes, or where it's all going. Simply read and chat and enjoy yourselves.

TIP: Listening in while reading along with your own copy of the work can help improve your concentration. Short stories are a really great route if you find that getting to the end of a full-blown novel is a little challenging.

Meditation: Energy Lightbulbs

(10 minutes)

This is a great meditation to do if flitting to and fro leaves you feeling low on energy. Here you can take a moment to gather yourself up, bringing all parts of yourself back to the here and now.

- Take an Easy Seat and a few nice Easy Breaths.
- Place one hand over your stomach and the other over your heart to get a sense of your body, the breath coming and going, and your heart beating.
- Imagine that you are wearing a hat decorated with many pretty lightbulbs.
- When you are focused on the now, the lightbulbs on that hat are all lighting up the present moment for you, clearly and brightly.
- However, some of these lightbulbs might be shining in different directions and lighting up someplace else. For example, they could be shining on a concern you have about work, the needs of your colleagues, the unknown nature of tonight's dinner or next year's summer holiday plans.
- Have a look and see if any of your lightbulbs are shining elsewhere. Using your imagination, begin to bring them back one by one so that they can glow within you, in the here and now.
- When you feel that the light from all your bulbs – and with it, all your attention – has been re-focused back inside you, take note of the sensation of being fully present in your current situation.
- Close your meditation with a few Easy Breaths.

THE AFTERNOON

After a busy morning and snatched lunch, the afternoon stretches ahead and it can be hard to keep motivated to get things done.

On the other hand, perhaps you spend your afternoons worrying that you are trying to pack in too much; you work obsessively and can't let go?

While these two behaviours seem contrary, they share one key similarity: avoidance. Avoidance is one of the psychological coping mechanisms we can become dependent upon in our lives. Alongside avoidance, there are several other key defence mechanisms our minds use in order to cope. These include: repression ('it never happened'), denial ('what never happened?'), projection ('I wish you'd stop doing that'), and rationalisation ('it was in the sale').

So how can we tackle avoidance and other unhelpful mechanisms, and enjoy getting the rest of our day's work done?

TIP: Towards the end of the afternoon, it can help to make a list of the work you intend to pick up again tomorrow. Make a note, and pop it away. Bookmark your day. Now you are ready for an evening of fun and exploration!

Get Naturally Disciplined with Tapas

The word *tapas* is Sanskrit for 'heat'. It is often associated with self-discipline or ascetic practices such as fasting, long meditations and going without home comforts in order to make oneself fit for spiritual growth.

I'm not really one for ascetic practices, I'm from Essex after all. And who needs to go out of their way to forge themselves in the furnace of austerity when everyday life situations (if bravely faced) offer all the character-building we could need?

All the same, welcoming uncomfortable feelings and sitting with them, as opposed to rejecting, denying or repressing them, can be a neat form of tapas.

TIP: Welcoming your fears or uncomfortable feelings doesn't necessarily mean they will automatically go away. But, whether they go away or not, they will slowly start to seem less of a bother.

Distraction Kit

(1 minute)

Have you noticed how ephemeral whims can be? They come and go so fleetingly. Oftentimes, we ourselves are left somewhat unclear as to what we really want in any given moment.

Try to spot this happening in your afternoon. You never know – despite your changing whims, you might find you are better able to resist distraction and get stuff done anyway.

The next time you spot an urge – for example, 'I think I'll go and make a cup of tea' – take a few moments to watch the urge without interfering.

- Rather than moving to fulfil the urge immediately, choose to sit with it for sixty seconds.
- Where does the urge appear? Is it in your body somewhere, or is it more of a mental process?
- As you watch, you might see how this urge at first appears and then evolves, eventually fading; at which point it may even be replaced by further ideas, feelings or urges.
- Having watched this process unfold, go ahead and choose what to do next. Whether to ignore it and keep on task, or to go ahead and fulfil it.
- Eventually you will be able to stay on task until it reaches its natural end or you reach your zenith.

Meditation: Laser-Sharp Focus

(15 seconds)

If left unchecked, we could all spend many minutes of the day following our thoughts as they meander along on a track of associations. How valuable it is, then, to learn about our minds – to refine our thinking and improve our capacity to pay attention.

Let's try something together, it's fun and it only takes a quarter of a minute:

- Sit back and let your thoughts run free, taking their full extension among the airwaves. Watch them for fifteen seconds, making a note of what you observe.

Studies have shown that people who meditate like this for just ten minutes a day make fewer task switches, and stay on task for longer, leading to an improved ability to sit down and get things done. The result is laser-sharp focus.

Being Patient

(5 minutes)

Something to consider: occasionally, if we put things off, they will eventually either get done by someone else, or disappear. Sometimes a little patience – or procrastination – can work in our favour.

The thinking mind is often relentlessly keen to progress. Sometimes this busyness is functional. However, we can get so used to being busy that we continue to generate task after task for ourselves – some of which may not be in our highest good.

This idea that procrastination is ok might sound unhelpful or even contradictory, because until now we have understood meditation as being a means of improving our focus and keeping us on task. Yet it can be good to acknowledge the endless preoccupation with doing that many of us have.

As your familiarity with your own procrastination habits deepens, you'll develop a heightened sensitivity to doing what feels right for you in any given work situation – be that to take it easy and be patient, or focus and get things done.

You are free to grow in the best way possible for you, even while you are knowingly procrastinating at work.

Meditation: The 4 p.m. *Al Desko*

(5 minutes)

This meditation is designed to help deal with stress and the feeling of being overwhelmed. (Sometimes before I practise it, I like to take off my shoes and glasses, and put on a cashmere jumper or something else lovely.)

Part One

- Sitting on your chair with your feet on the ground and back straight, take an Easy Breath.
- Close your eyes and perhaps plug in your headphones if you might be interrupted by a friendly colleague.
- Acknowledge and accept your current situation (that means all your thoughts, feelings, emotions as well as external things like sounds and smells).
- Take note of what is happening that makes you think you are stressed. Break the word 'stress' down into its raw components. For example, maybe there might be heat, tension, tingling, racing thoughts or a hunger.

Part Two

- Breathe in through your nose for roughly seven counts, and breathe out for roughly eleven counts. You can count on your fingers if it helps. But there's no need to try too hard to keep to this pattern.

- After a few minutes close with a mantra. My personal favourite that I use for my classes is: 'Right now, right here, in this moment, everything is ok.' You can repeat that mantra a few times in your mind or out loud if you want to lighten the mood at work.

TIP: Go out with a bang. Bookend your five-minute breathing meditation by listening to your favourite happy-song via headphones. Pick a song that, for you, really embodies a relaxed, uplifting sentiment.

Loving Your Work

One day the word 'work' will become obsolete.

I like to think that a time will come when people will be able to do the work they enjoy and are good at – to the effect that there will be no more work, *per se*, there will just be living. Probably there will be activity still, but it will be done for its own sake and won't be seen as work in the way this is conventionally considered. Perhaps I'm being a little fanciful, but that is what I hope for us . . .

No, it definitely still feels like work!

Ok, if you can't love it, at least accept your work and be grateful for the beer money. If you treat what you are doing well, a subtle shift might take place in your mindset from disillusionment and resistance to gratitude and presence that will open new doors for you. Plus, you'll have more fun while you're there – and who wants to be miserable anyway?

TIP: Read 'It Couldn't Be Done', a totally amazing poem by Edgar Albert Guest.

POST-WORK DETOX

A NIGHT AT HOME: enjoy five to ten minutes of Switch Off From Work Meditation with a cup of peppermint tea.

EXERCISE: follow with some light stretches and an inspiring, creative activity such as letter writing.

CONNECT: spend time with others celebrating life and having fun. Make the OH Mantra for Feeling Confident and in the Middle and grow familiar with your own voice; feel happy being who you are – everyone flowers differently.

MINDFUL EATING: shop for healthy, nutritious foods that make you feel great. Prepare a meal with love and eat mindfully, savouring every mouthful.

GETTING READY FOR BED: spritz your bedroom with aromatherapy oils and make a chamomile and lavender tea. Read a great novel or listen to a beautiful piece of music.

DRIFT OFF: close your eyes and review your day; from your freshly woken moment this morning, through to climbing into bed just a minute or two ago. Take three Easy Breaths, in and out, and drift off into a deep nourishing sleep.

HOME TIME

It can be an obvious shift that occurs as the clock strikes 5 p.m., or during the commute. For some of us, especially perhaps for those of us working at home, the transition from work to leisure is more nuanced, an inner reorientation and a gentle sense of closure.

Knowingly or unknowingly, we need our little rituals to help us lay the day's work to rest. Once we find ways to switch off, the evening can become a sanctuary – a time to recuperate from the day and prepare for the next one.

What's more, the evening is to be enjoyed for its own sake. More than just a slither of unusable time between work days, it can be your opportunity to explore your happiness outside the boundaries of your usual wage-earning work.

Let's commit to valuing our evening time so that we can make the very best use of it! Responsibilities and commitments allowing, we have several hours between now and bedtime – so what is the thing you would most like to be doing?

As well as being an opportunity for fun activities, like letter writing and spa treats, nights at home thankfully offer us the chance to just be.

Workaholism

As I was leaving my office at around 5 p.m. one afternoon, someone called out, 'Half day?' However, despite our workhorse culture, there is a growing body of evidence to suggest that – for all our good intentions – working too hard doesn't do us or quality of the work itself any favours.

Erin Reid, a professor at Boston University, found that managers were unable to tell, based on output, which employees had worked eighty hours and which were just pretending to work. If we are low on energy it can seriously impair our interpersonal skills too. Making judgement calls, reading other people's faces, managing our own emotional reactions and communication all appear to suffer in response to stress and over-working. Just like children, we get tired and cranky, making it increasingly difficult to act in line with our usual love and understanding.

TIP: You aren't a commodity, you're an artist – and just like completing a beautiful painting, you've got to know when a day's work is done!

Creating a Working Balance

Don't confuse activity with achievement: studies suggest that some people waste around two hours every eight-hour day at work making personal calls and doing other (self-preserving) activities like surfing the web and making coffee. Many companies are coming round to the idea that, if given the opportunity, office staff would work productively for four days, and enjoy the fifth off. Here are some survival tips:

Reframe Your Leisure Time

Sometimes we are so passionate about our work that we want to give it our all – and any time spent away from our business can feel guilt-provoking. If this applies to you, I would like to invite you to do a little investigation here, and see whether or not reclaiming your post-work period influences the quality of your work during the day.

Disco Naps

Research involving almost 400 middle-aged men and women suggests that those who took naps at lunch time reported lower blood pressure than those who stayed awake the whole day through.

Work with your own rhythm: some days you might be very creative and other days you might be quieter. Such is the natural flow of life.

Give Your Brain a Rest

I have a friend who says he needs to 'come away from things' during the day, but he can't seem to meditate at the office. We explored other activities he could do during lunch and he decided to learn French. After ten minutes at lunchtime conjugating verbs, he now feels calmer and refreshed.

The Pit Stop

When was the last time you ate something wholesome and nutritious? If it was hours ago, why not try picking up some fruit or a heathy snack on the way home so you aren't ravenous when you walk through the door?

Meditation: Switch Off From Work

(8 minutes)

Take an Easy Seat.
Follow your Easy Breath for a few moments.
Let your body settle in.
Take a little journey in your imagination. (Some people use their inner vision to see themselves doing particular things on their way home, for instance.)

Imagine that you are now making your way to your wardrobe.
It's been a long day and so much has passed ...
Piece by piece, begin to take off your working clothes really thoughtfully, thankful for the things they have seen with you during the day.
Hang up each piece carefully.
Feeling lighter with each item you take off.

Close the wardrobe.

Give it a moment and open the wardrobe again – and you'll be amazed to find a whole other selection of clothes at your disposal.
Piece by piece, begin re-dressing.
Feel yourself shifting your perspective and beginning afresh. A new day.
Close the wardrobe and make your way back, in your imagination, to the here and now, in your body, resting, fresh, clean and ready to begin a new part of your day.

EVENINGS IN

If we have responsibilities, of course we need to manage those as best we can. That said, it's interesting how the mind is never quite satisfied with what is: if we're in, we should be out; if we're out, we should be in. If we're without children, we want them; if we've got them, we crave five minutes to ourselves. If we're single, we should have someone ... and so it goes on.

You don't always have to listen to the judgements of your mind – it might lead you in circles. If you fancy an evening in, make the most of it.

Self-Care as an Expression of Love

When you are healthy, happy and vibrant you are likely to live from a place of fullness – and be a great contributor to the world in whichever way you can be.

It's when you stop taking care of yourself and your needs that the finger-pointing usually starts. Not only might you be less able to help others, but you may be more likely to blame them for your discontent and start making demands on them to fix it – demands that are simply not feasible.

Other people don't know how to tend your patch of land, not really. They probably have enough to deal with, looking after their own.

Self-care isn't selfish. The way you regard yourself is often how you treat the world, and so to explore your happiness is truly a lovely thing.

Meditation: Exploring Self-Care

(3 minutes)

Take an Easy Seat and adopt the Ready position.

Take five Easy Breaths.

Take a few moments to scan through your body quickly to see how it is doing. Listen to your hips, feet and arms; how do they feel right now?

Close your meditation by asking the question, 'What form does my self-care want to take, right now?'

TIP: Self-care changes shape in line with your needs in any given moment.

Just Being a Hermit

It is easy to become distracted from our good intentions by the interactions and storylines we share with others. Time alone gives us a chance to focus inwardly and think for ourselves.

When you spend time alone, you'll get to know your own fragrance. When alone, you can't attribute your internal condition to anyone else.

Throughout history, there are stories of well-respected spiritual figures disappearing off by themselves at what seem to have been formative periods in their lives.

Enjoy some time alone and see where this leads you.

Meditation: Just Being

(5 minutes)

For some, being alone can take a little getting used to. If you have just five minutes to yourself of an evening, try this simple Just Being Meditation.

- Find a comfortable place to sit down in your Easy Seat.
- Put away anything that might normally keep you occupied. For example, a phone or a book.
- Approach the next five minutes free from all motive. There is nothing pre-determined to achieve or get done here.
- You aren't directing your attention in one direction or another and so it can freely evolve.
- Notice whatever you notice as things come and go.
- Happily, you may well relax, or even find yourself re-energised – but whatever comes, you are content to spend five minutes *just being*.
- If you remain unoccupied like this, the meditation will thrive of its own accord without much effort.

TIP: Sometimes it's nice to just be. Nowhere to go, nothing to do. The trick is to remain unoccupied during your five free minutes. Some people discover that when they are blessed with a good slot of time – the stuff of *just-being* dreams – they find themselves just having to do this, or just having to do that, and so they lose their 'me' time. If we aren't careful we might even end up blaming someone else for this.

Just Playing

(10 minutes)

Anyone who has watched children transporting sand from one corner of the beach to the other – and back again – may be familiar with a joyful display of play that is often both spontaneous and without purpose. There's no point to it. Or rather there is a point and that point is fun.

Find ten minutes tonight to play. It could be with your pets or with maths equations, with colouring pens or playing with the plants. No ambition is involved, no need to be improving or accruing or getting somewhere. Pure unadulterated, senseless fun.

A Mini Digital Detox

(A few hours)

How many doses of digital data do you receive a week?

It's possible to lose hours in endless timelines as we skim down pages such as Facebook, Twitter and other online platforms. Social media often seems addictive and can pull us away from the stuff of our life and into some other place – but there's more to a digital detox than curbing your Instagram fix.

Taking time out will help us develop greater awareness of the subtle ideals that digital media might be propagating within us.

Social media, online TV, radio, streaming music? Which of these influences might you include in a digital detox?

Take a break from the screen. Try 'no devices after 7 p.m.' or even 'no-TV Tuesdays'.

Meditation: The Inner Detox

(15 minutes)

This is a great meditation for those times where you feel full of other people's influence. You want to clear those ideas out and feel more like you again.

Here's how to get started:

- Lay down somewhere safe and relaxing. Close your eyes, making sure your head and neck are supported comfortably.
- Take five Easy Breaths in through the nose and out through the nose.
- Imagine that you have a magic vacuum cleaner and, as you pass it around your body, from the tips of your toes to the top of your head, it removes all the residue of the day, including any ideas, preoccupations and influences from the media.
- Take all the time you need in the next few moments to pass that vacuum cleaner around your body. Remember to do it with a sense of attentiveness, listening out for those parts of the body that might be carrying a heavier load.
- Travel through the body, gently noting all the influences, sensations or feelings that are being removed and feel yourself getting lighter with each breath.
- Close with a few Easy Breaths in and out.

A False Reality

Here's something to ponder on: back in the 1980s, French philosopher Jean Baudrillard used the term 'the Simulacrum' to describe the false copy of reality presented by the media. Today, the online profiles and digital images that were once made to represent reality now mask it, with the viewer slowly beginning to mistake the map (the image) for the terrain (the real person) it was built to represent.

This reminds me how important it is to recognise that digital media is not the Gospel. Just because you've seen it in a video or someone tweeted it, doesn't make it real. The representation of reality you are offered online may not be accurate.

Ultimately, what you take to be true will be down to you ...

TIP: Read *The Ecstasy of Communication* by Jean Baudrillard.

Things to Love about the Internet

Of course, spending time online can have many benefits too, when it's all part of a healthy balance.

IDENTITY EXPLORATION: creating boards, pages and picture collections as a way of exploring the different sides of your personality, and finding new strengths and joys.

CREATIVITY: designing images, creating playlists and garnering new ideas.

LEARNING AND SHARING: lots of courses and information are available online from all kinds of people around the world.

CONNECTING: connecting with people who share your interests so, regardless of how niche your hobbies are, you are no longer limited to your home town.

OPPORTUNITY: the internet can open a door to those of us who might previously have felt isolated and cut off from the world.

Letter Writing

Just lately my friend asked for my postal address as she wanted to write me an old-fashioned letter.

'You don't have to write one back,' she assured me.

I received her letter in the post some time later. It was complete with illustrations and was a joy to read. Almost as though she had sprinkled a little bit of herself in an envelope and sent it to me. And, even better, the onus to reply had been lifted.

Sitting down to pen a letter to a friend the old-fashioned way can be a lovely means to stay in touch, and a great excuse to take a few minutes out at the end of the day.

Meditation: Write a Letter to a Friend

(10 minutes to 1 hour)

Prepare a Space

Make a space in your living area and set aside enough time for what you want to say. Perhaps light a scented candle or spray fragrance. You can be quite creative with stationery: handmade paper is lovely, as are fragranced paper and beautiful envelopes.

Prepare Yourself

Start your letter writing with a few minutes of meditation. With your eyes closed, take a few Easy Breaths and come to the Middle. Really gather yourself up, be patient as you arrive in the moment, fully here, fully into whatever it is you are about to do.

And Write . . .

Just start writing. Be aware of any strict ideas lurking around as to what you believe needs to go into a letter, such as letters have to be long, eloquent, short, witty or probing . . . Instead, just see what wants to be written and go with the flow.

EVENINGS OUT

Evenings out can represent an active choice to seek out the company of people who share the same interests as yourself, such as salsa dancing, ice skating or a love of meditational things.

Or perhaps you are interested in discovering the new worlds out there and the people who inhabit them? If this wish is in you authentically, you will likely find that it fulfils itself quite serendipitously.

We all share something of a common essence and ultimately this is what we enjoy when we spend time with other people. Whatever it is in you that is aware of these words, dear reader, is also in me, aware of them too ...

Sometimes, though, we can underestimate the qualities we bring to the party, and that's why I'm going to look at what we mean by self-esteem in this chapter. Whatever company you find yourself in, there is a part for you to play whether or not you realise it.

TIP: Visit a public park and take a walk around trying not to influence anyone.

Mirror Explorations

(2 minutes)

It's quite a funny thing to look in the mirror. People often look in them absentmindedly. 'That's me!' you might say, albeit unconsciously, as you tidy your fringe. But is it true?

Consider bringing a little added presence to your mirror experience by becoming aware of how you interact with your perceived image.

Try these explorative questions:

- What can I see?
- What kind of judgements or interpretations do I make about my appearance?

If there is an opinion that arises in response to what you see, try not to focus on the content of it too much; instead enquire as to who it is that has the opinion.

TIP: Write on your mirror using lipstick, or impermanent ink, a few verses from the love poetry of D. H. Lawrence.

Compliments

Here's something I often hear when I'm teaching meditation: '*I don't always like what I see, and I find it hard to get past that, let alone be mindful. Help!*'

When we're feeling good, we usually feel that we look good too. Someone once told me that it's a wise idea to stand in front of the mirror and pay yourself one genuine compliment a day. This works especially well if you're feeling a bit fed up. But it's got to be a compliment that you can actually believe – or at least something you could get halfway behind.

Friendly Feedback

(10 minutes)

If you can't think of something nice to say to your reflection, why not ask a friend? Or ask several of the people you know who care about you to share six things (adjectives, phrases, qualities) that they most enjoy or admire about you. You might be pleasantly surprised.

Everyone flowers differently and we all have something beautiful about us. Note these key words and phrases down in your journal alongside the other inspiring insights you have collected throughout your day.

Self-Talk

Notice the quality of your self-talk. Is it filled with self-doubt or put-downs? Self-talk shows up as a kind of internalised running commentary, an interpretation of what's happening.

The way we interpret things is massively altered by our current state of consciousness. This is ever more apparent if you have ever had a few too many espresso martinis or, as a woman, experienced PMS.

TIP: Still struggling to find a positive slant? Try affirming this mantra: 'Today I choose to see myself with love.' And when you say 'myself' be sure to mean all of your feelings, interpretations and thoughts.

Exploring and Re-interpreting Your Self-Image

(10 minutes)

Who we think we are influences our choices and sense of wellbeing. For example, if you see yourself as a successful and dedicated athlete it may then feel natural and easy to by-pass the fast food shop on your way home, because you are very aware that successful athletes 'just don't do that sort of thing'.

Exploring your self-image can be very illuminating. You might start with making notes in your journal for ten minutes on questions such as: 'Who do I take myself for?' and 'Does my self-image limit me or empower me now?'

TIP: Read the poem 'I know the Way You can Get' by Hafiz (which is totally wow!).

Am I Bianca Jagger?

One day I decided that in order to explore myself I would pretend to be someone else for a few hours. And so the 'Who am I, Am I Bianca Jagger?' meditation was born.

My friend collected me and together we went to visit to the Saatchi Gallery in London. Before we set out, I decided that I would do all the things I'd normally do that day – but I would do them all as Bianca Jagger, the former actress and human rights advocate. I'd eat like Bianca Jagger, get dressed like Bianca Jagger and meet friends as Bianca Jagger.

And it was great. Nothing much changed in my outward behaviour, but the shift in my self-concept adjusted my approach to life a little. For example, I ate my toast differently. Took a little more care over choosing my outfit. Strode out to the car in my sunnies more confidently. Mooched around the paintings – thrilled that I'd managed to go to the art gallery without getting papped. At some point the novelty wore off and I was back to being me.

Here's What I Uncovered

- My behaviours and expectations match the current sense of self I'm entertaining.
- Picking a character that wasn't me created a helpful perspective on who I really am. Sometimes our sense of self is such a tacit assumption that it's not always easy to see it in action, whereas behaving like somebody else provides an insightful contrast.
- The experience unlocked capacities and tendencies in me that were not so readily available in my behavioural repertoire as Emma Mills. Like talking loudly and confidently, wearing sunglasses all the time or feeling I belonged to the jet set!

Afterwards, I sat in the art gallery and contemplated a new twist on an ancient meditation question:

Who am I?
(Am I Bianca Jagger?)

Meditation: Who Am I – Bianca Jagger?

(An hour or so, time and enthusiasm permitting)

Try your own version of this meditation out for size. Maybe you'll pick a different person when you follow the imaginative exercise I've described above.

- So who do you want to be for your evening out – or perhaps for your whole day?
- Make a note of your discoveries in your journal.

Having True Self-Esteem

The term 'self-esteem' is used to describe a person's overall sense of personal value. Yet this self, around which our perceived worth revolves, changes quite a bit. For example, early on in life we might think of ourselves as a young child, yet as time passes perhaps we begin to change our self-image and see ourselves as being more mature.

What's more, the sense of self we entertain is often highly influenced by what we believe others think of us, and the changing feedback we've received from them over the years.

Having made a few enquiries and gained a clearer view of the self-concept that operates within us, we can, if we like, undertake to nurture ourselves a little and improve our self-esteem.

It can be very worthwhile to do this, and to get to know our character at the same time; yet we shouldn't get bogged down in this identity alone – we are much more than just our personality.

Meditation: Recognising Our True Self-Worth

(7 minutes)

There is a sense of self referred to in many meditative traditions – our presence – that can also be loved and attended to.

It's difficult to define precisely what that presence is, as it lacks objective qualities. The good news is that we don't need to define it. We can, however, become increasingly aware of it through meditation. Hurrah!

Here's a really lovely practice to explore before going out one evening, when you have a little time and enthusiasm.

- Take an Easy Seat and close your eyes.
- Take ten Easy Breaths and adopt the Ready position.
- Inwardly ask the question: 'What is it that is aware of this inhale, exhale rhythm?'
- Sit with this question for a few moments exploring any ideas, notions or knowings that come to you. It isn't necessary to come up with a concrete answer here; it may be that you get a sense of something without necessarily having to go further.
- When you feel ready, let the question drift away and begin to pay attention to all and any sensations in your hands or feet, feeling the energy that moves through your body as you rest quietly where you are.
- Follow this sensation as it moves and evolves within the body for a further few minutes.
- Close the meditation with a few Easy Breaths.

Meditation: A Mantra for Feeling Confident and in the Middle

(3 minutes)

So you have decided to go out for the night. You arrive at a party and you feel out of sorts, full of social jitters. You don't know what to do with your hands and your arms seem a million miles long.

Take a good look round the room. Nearly everybody there will have felt like you do at some point. So even when you feel awkward and alone, you're not really – there are other people who feel just like you.

This is a great meditation for these situations. If possible, practise it before a night out or alternatively find a quiet and relatively private spot at the party, and give it a go!

- Take an Easy Seat and help your body to become nice and comfortable, making sure that your breathing is free and unrestricted.
- Close your eyes and place a hand over your stomach.
- Take a few Easy Breaths in and out through your nose.
- When you feel ready, make the sound *'oh'* on your next out-breath. 'Oh' as it is sounded in the words 'home' or 'omnipresent'.
- Repeat the 'oh' sound on each out-breath for ten breaths. Remember not to rush, treat each 'oh' as though it were the only 'oh'.
- Once complete, sit quietly for sixty seconds or so while that vibration settles.

Thriving in Social Occasions

Some of our social woes are exacerbated by our thought processes and our fantasies about what others think of us, as well as our efforts to have them think of us in a certain way. This can be tricky – I mean, who of us here doesn't want to be liked, honestly? And yet it might be nice to give the other person the freedom to make of us whatever they will, and for us too to enjoy that liberty.

Something to consider: if you are busy talking to yourself it's tricky to listen to others properly. Be generous and pay attention to the other person, replacing your concern with how you are coming across with a desire to listen.

TIP: Don't worry if it takes time for you to feel comfortable with this. We all have obstacles to overcome. However, if you find this area particularly bothersome, it might help to explore your feelings with the help of a therapist or a coach.

Meditation: the Voyeur Partner

(10 minutes)

Here's a lovely meditation to do with friends. It's so refreshing to sit down and be present with one another, with no intentions or demands.

- Friends A and B sit opposite each other on chairs, setting a timer for five minutes.
- Friend A: close your eyes, settle down and enjoy some easy breathing.
- Friend B: watch Friend A as they sit there breathing gently. Simply allow them to be as they are. Perhaps start by noticing the signs of their breathing. Not wanting anything from them, liking or disliking, wanting them to be different, to relax or to do a certain thing. Just be the accepting witness of their being.
- When the timer buzzes, close by thanking your friend and then switch roles.

(This is also a fun meditation to do with a romantic partner.)

Choosing in Line with Happiness

(10 minutes)

Sometimes it can feel hard to decide how to spend your precious evenings out, especially if there is a lot on offer! Try this exercise to help you choose in line with happiness.

Begin by identifying the qualities in life that are truly important to you (for example, love, generosity, novelty, connecting, cleanliness, beauty, communication, learning). If you are unsure of the qualities you enjoy most, it can help to look closely at the hobbies, pasttimes, people or films you really love, and then explore what it is exactly you enjoy about these things.

- Make a list of these qualities in your journal.
- With this list to hand, it can be easier to choose how to spend your spare time and money, based on how well they fit with your highest qualities.

DINNER

Our evening meal is a chance to sit down, and celebrate. (Yes! Another day under our belt!) If we have the chance, sharing a meal socially can be a great way to feel connected with others. It's also a lovely opportunity to pick up foodie inspiration.

Dining alone can be equally enriching. In the quietness of our own company, we can take our time to choose what we eat thoughtfully, in line with our body's needs.

In Part One, we touched upon the mind's limited capacity to conceive completely new concepts. However, for quite some distance along the path of self-understanding, the mind is the key tool we have at our disposal. It is therefore crucial to consume foods that are conducive to our mental clarity. Rather than offering specific food recommendations in this chapter, the focus will be on enhancing your sensitivity to flavours and foodstuffs so you can choose foods that feel amazing to eat.

GET SENSITISED: enhance your appreciation of food by spending five minutes practising the Undressed Banana Meditation (see page 119).

FOOD SHOP: head out with your healthiest self in mind and shop for ingredients that are fun to cook and offer the greatest good.

PREPARATION: Take a moment to note all of the wonderful smells, textures and colours available in the moment, observing how they evolve during the cooking process.

118 INHALE · EXHALE · REPEAT

SITTING DOWN TO DINE: enjoy a few Easy Breaths before you begin your meal.

GO GENTLY: take the time to really relish each spoonful. Pop your cutlery down between mouthfuls so that you can appreciate each bite.

AFTER DINNER: in the time that follows your meal be sure to reflect on how the food you have eaten has contributed to your wellbeing.

TEA: close with a soothing cup of peppermint tea.

TIP: You might like to set a positive intention for your mealtime, for example, 'Let this food keep me strong and healthy.'

Meditation: The Undressed Banana

(5 minutes)

Do this meditation before you set out to the shops. It can help you to cultivate your sensitivity or intuition so you can see how you respond to certain foods.

Ok, here goes:

- Take a banana. Sit in front of it. Hold it. Feel it. Put it down.
- Now, remove the label 'banana' from it.
- If in your mind you look and say, 'Banana,' now look and don't say anything. Just experience it as it is.
- Sit with it.

This meditation might sound hilarious or ridiculous, but I promise there are goodies here. Through this exercise, we learn to experience the 'beingness' of the banana: seeing the reality of it, seeing it as it is, rather than a concept based on our memories and preconceptions of bananas.

With time, we might extend this ability to perceive the 'beingness' of things to our friends and loved ones too.

Getting Ready To Shop

Having made your shopping list, it's time to prepare for your shop symbolically:

Option One

(1 hour)

You've got ages. A lazy Sunday morning, or a Friday evening are perfect for leisurely shopping.

You're about to shop for food with your highest love and understanding in mind. You are intending to listen to your inner self, and spend time buying just the right things to nourish and fulfil you. To generate new cells and new blood.

Why not dress for the occasion and take time to put on something that inspires you? Something that, whenever you wear it, you are prone to having loving ideas about yourself. Ideas that are in line with your new mindful way of life. You might even do your hair too. This is an invitation to wear something that enlivens your sense of healthy eating.

Option Two

(5 minutes)

You've got no time, literally – you needed this shop yesterday. All the same, wash your face and hands, put on a spritz of cologne and a fresh jersey. Prepare yourself to make healthy choices.

Mindful Eating

Here are five key ways to apply a mindful living ethos to your mealtimes.

1.   RELISH: once it's eaten, it's eaten – so take your time and savour every morsel without rushing to the end too quickly.

2.   NOTICE: explore the many sights, sounds, smells, tastes and textures of your food. Switch off the television and the smartphone so that you can give eating your full attention.

3.   CELEBRATE: approach the plate, the knife and the spoon with revelry, and gratitude. This way, eating can become a celebration of life.

4.   SHARE: take the opportunity to share your food with a friend or loved one. Eating together mindfully can be both a celebration and a reminder of your shared humanity. Here you both are, doing something people have done for millions of years. How very normal and reassuring. (By the way, when I gobble my dinner down, I notice my friend miraculously starts following suit. Staying present at mealtime, even if in company, helps me manage my own rhythm.)

5.   RELAX: take five minutes before you start eating to do a simple breathing meditation. At best, you'll feel a little lighter afterwards, and at the very least you'll be a little more connected to your body's needs.

Enough Is Enough

(60 seconds)

Sometimes food can be so tasty, though. It can be easy to overfill the plate, especially at key trigger times such as Christmas, holidays, birthdays or days of the week that end in 'y'.

If you have found portion control, calorie counting and willpower to be less than entirely helpful in your bid to stop overeating, why not experiment with a little surrender?

Not many people like being told what to do. Some people even find that the moment they aren't supposed to be doing something, it suddenly becomes essential. Usually, if you think you shouldn't be doing something (like overeating) you will likely try to do it quickly in a kind of food trance, or in a semi-secretive fashion to avoid the dissonance that goes with doing something you've judged to be bad.

Have you seen this happen? If this sounds like you, then why not let go of any prejudices you have as to what you will eat, and ease up on the reins a little. It doesn't mean that you go out and eat any old rubbish, but try giving yourself full permission in the moment to listen to your body.

Sometimes Science Can Really Help

Are there some foods that feel better to you than others?

Sometimes a certain type of food feels good in the moment, but then it doesn't agree with us in the days that follow. Mindful eating is about calm, conscious eating, and it is also about developing a continued sensitivity towards the ways that food influences your wellbeing in the days that follow your meal. (Be aware, though, that a meditative approach to food shouldn't replace or exclude the guidance of a qualified healthcare professional.)

TIP: Take five minutes each day to note your foodie reflections in your journal.

Food to Share

Here're a couple of perfect recipes to share around the table or to keep in the fridge to use in your work lunchboxes.

The English Garden

Serves 2

1 tbsp coconut oil
1 handful curly kale
1 handful broccoli florets
½ courgette, sliced into thin sticks
2 garlic cloves, chopped
2 small spring onions, chopped
1 small knob of ginger, finely chopped
1 handful fresh peas
¼ small leek, finely chopped.
Several basil leaves, chopped
1 poached egg (e.g. organic free-range duck egg)

Method: lightly stir-fry all the ingredients, except the egg, in the coconut oil for around eight to ten minutes or until the vegetables soften. When the green vegetables are as soft as you'd like them to be, tip them into a bowl. Pop a poached egg on top and serve with a few fresh basil leaves.

TIP: This meal reminds me of the English countryside as described by John Clare in his poems. Lots of luscious green and sweet peas and rogue hens running around the place.

Persian Pearls

I love this simple, fruity dish. Basically, it's quinoa with multi-coloured dried fruits and vegetable 'pearls'. When served in a big bowl, it looks as though you've just taken a scoop from a gem-peppered treasure trove, released from deep under the earth. Which, when you think about it, you have!

Serves 3 (2 for dinner, and 1 for lunch the next day!)

½ cup quinoa
1 cup water for cooking the quinoa
1 handful pistachios
1 handful dried cranberries
1 handful fresh blueberries
1 large carrot, chopped into small, slim sticks
6 yellow baby tomatoes or 15 dried mango pieces
Seeds of ½ pomegranate
A tiny pinch of cinnamon, turmeric and ground cardamom
½ cup white beans, cooked
½ tsp brown sugar

Method: cook the quinoa according to the instructions on the pack in the boiling water. When ready, remove from the heat and drain the water. Immediately stir the other ingredients into the pot and place the lid on so as to allow it to steam and cool naturally. Serve with a handful of finely chopped fresh flat leaf parsley.

Moonlit Soup

This filling soup cooks quickly and freezes well, which can be really handy if you need to rustle up a wholesome meal late one evening.

Serves 2

1 red onion, finely chopped
3 garlic cloves, finely chopped
1 green chili pepper, finely chopped
2 sticks celery, chopped
1 carrot, chopped
1 tbsp coconut oil
2 cups black beans, cooked
3 cherry tomatoes, chopped
1 cup vegetable stock
1 tbsp chia seeds
1 cup water
Black pepper, to taste
Himalayan pink salt, to taste
2 tbsp crème fraîche, scoop of avocado or 2 poached eggs, to serve
Sprinkling of fresh coriander, chopped, to serve

Method: sauté the onion, garlic, chilli, celery and carrot in a pan in the coconut oil for five minutes until tender. Add the cooked black beans, chopped tomatoes and vegetable stock. Simmer for a further five minutes. Add the chia seeds. Blend the mix until smooth, adding water to taste. Season with plenty of black pepper and Himalayan pink salt to taste. Complete this dark, rich soup by adding either a poached egg, a scoop of avocado, or a dollop of crème fraiche, and a sprinkling of coriander on top to serve.

TIP: Read the short poem 'The Listeners' by Walter De La Mare and imagine all the people around the world, travelling by moonlight tonight!

BEDTIME

So you've spent a relaxing evening at home, or perhaps you've been out and about with friends. Either way, it's a good idea to spend a little time winding down before you go to bed.

As you might have guessed, I enjoy a good book before bedtime, and I also find that music can be soothing before I go to sleep. Here are some suggestions for ways to end the day peacefully, ready to enjoy a good night's sleep.

TIP: Bringing your phone to the bedroom could influence your relationships. In a recent study, over half of the female participants said their relationships suffered because their partner was distracted by their phone during 'couple leisure time', otherwise known as the time when couples actually interact in real life.

Music for the Mind

Consider the music you listen to at home of an evening. Does it gets you all riled up, or make you sleepy? Maybe it's priming you to behave in a particular way.

I've noticed that if I listen to my favourite jazz singer while trying to work on my art portfolio in the evening, my inner orientation becomes one of '*mañana mañana*, what's the rush?'

Whereas certain rap songs encourage my ambition and drive: 'Got to grind hard and make it out of the ghetto!'

Self-awareness can make listening to music extra enriching. Take a little time to think about how your favourite music really makes you feel tonight.

Meditation: Music Night

(3 minutes, or the length of your song)

How lovely to sit and play a song (or an album) and listen properly to it the whole way through, rather than having it on in the background while you do something else . . .

- Cue up your song and dim the lights.
- Sit, or lay, and listen with the whole body.
- Stay gently alert (as with the I'm Listening Pose) rather than snoozing.
- Explore the rhythm, the way it peaks and troughs, the tones and the words.
- Enjoy being present with the music.
- Notice the feelings and sensations it evokes in you.

Intentional Reading

(20 minutes)

PICK A PARTICULAR SHORT STORY OR NOVEL: choose a work that encompasses themes you want to improve your understanding of. For example, themes such as leadership, forgiveness, or sensuality. Remember to pause for reflection every now and then as you explore the themes and ideas that are being offered in the book or story. Perhaps it approaches life from an angle you'd not considered before.

SHARED READING: it's interesting to see how people can interpret the same passage so differently. At times, this discrepancy highlights our own interpretational bias and patterns. Observing this in action is a totally wow moment. Poems in particular can act as a kind of literary inkblot test of a person's mental orientation.

COMPLEX CHARACTERS: don't underestimate the power of fiction. Reading classical literature filled with complex characters is challenging to our brains, which can otherwise become used to anticipating certain behaviour patterns from particular types of people.

TIP: Try reading the works of Doris Lessing for rites of passage, H. G. Wells for insights into the human condition, Chekhov for social consciousness, Philip K. Dick for imagination and O. Henry for love conundrums.

Keeping a Diary

Traditionally you might recount the day's experiences in a diary, but there are many other diary styles. For example, why not try:

- Recounting your day backwards.
- Recounting the colours you saw.
- Recounting your blessings.
- Recounting the ways you used your skills and strengths.
- Recounting the day from another person's perspective.

Lavender and Chamomile Tea

(4 minutes)

Add a teaspoon of chamomile flowers and a teaspoon of lavender to a teapot of hot water. Allow to steep for 3 minutes.

Serve with a slice of lemon and enjoy!

Meditation: Home Spa Night

(45 minutes)

Oh, how delightful it is to saunter down to the bathing shed with one's glass of vodka for an evening swim among the nodding waterweeds! Ok, so it's not the 1890s and we aren't in a Russian fairy tale, but you can't beat a nice bath for a little luxury me-time.

All you need is: bubble bath + a beautiful fragrance + a tall glass of water with a slice of cucumber.

Home spa time can be a wonderful exercise in sensuality. But what do I mean – meditation? At bath time? Is nothing sacred these days!

I'm not wanting to turn everything you do into an exercise, honest – especially while you are trying to relax – but bath time does seem like the perfect place to explore the sensual part of your experience:

- As you lie there, become aware of your body.
- Engage the senses.
- Watch sensations emerge, unfold and dissolve.

Afterwards, treat yourself to some soft new socks or a good book, and to all extents and purposes pamper yourself like you mean it.

TIP: Try adding Epsom salts or bentonite clay to your bath for an added cleanse. If you mix the bentonite clay up with a little water it makes a good face mask too.

Meditation: Moisturising

(5 minutes)

Here's a meditation you can do to feel truly at ease in your own skin while pampering yourself.

- Take a dollop of your favourite body moisturiser.
- As you massage the cream into your feet say to yourself, 'These are my feet.'
- As you massage your legs say, 'These are my legs.'
- As you massage your arms, say, 'These are my arms.'
- Continue to acknowledge your body as you massage the cream into different parts of it.

If you don't moisturise, you can try the same exercise by gently tapping your palms over each part of the body, again saying, 'These are my thighs, these are my elbows,' etc.

This practice brings awareness to different parts of the body, lighting up their corresponding counterparts in the brain. It will also put you in touch with your sensual self, your body and presence.

Meditation: Preparing for a Great Night's Sleep

(10 minutes)

This is a really lovely meditation to do if you find it tricky to leave your daily concerns behind when heading to bed. You can do it lying down in bed or as part of a pre-bed meditation, sitting in your Easy Seat. Here's how to get started:

- Let your eyes become gentle and unfocused, the way you would look at a person you love or are fond of – the opposite of starting intently.
- Take five Easy Breaths in and out, and then let your eyes close.
- Observe whatever is happening in your thinking and bodily experience this very moment (thoughts, memories, feelings and sensations such as tiredness, for example).
- Try to consider these happenings impartially, without identifying with them. For example, rather than being restless, observe that restlessness is happening.
- Imagine your attention to be like a hot sun, and your restlessness, or other concerns, are like little puddles: as your attention shines on them, they gradually evaporate.
- When you have explored all the happenings that present themselves to you this bedtime, close your eyes and drift into restful sleep.

Lights Out Routine

Turn off devices and electronics in good time.

Practise five or ten minutes of evening meditation.

Prepare a nice herbal tea; at this hour, I like to drink chamomile tea, which I grow in a pot on my windowsill.

Spritz your pillows with an aromatherapy spray, such as lavender or rosewood.

Having enjoyed a soothing bath, climb into bed and read a few passages from a spiritual book. I prefer not to read anything too racy, such as a thrilling novel or a rapturous poem, before lights out. Instead, I tend to go for something uplifting and feel-good. For you, a relaxing read might be something else.

Fall asleep with your mind dwelling on goodness.

Meditation: Drifting Off

(1 to 5 minutes)

This meditation only takes ten breaths, but you can repeat the sequence until you feel yourself sink into sleep. As you lie quietly in your bed, feeling your body against the sheets and the weight of your body being supported by the bed, count your breathing up to ten as you breathe in, and again, as you breathe out.

Meditation: the Witching Hour

(6 minutes)

It's the middle of the night, everyone around you is fast asleep, yet here you are – wide awake and aware of the night at large.

Think of all the brains and nervous systems that usually function so rapidly around you during the day – all currently switched to delta brain waves, the frequency of deep sleep. Imagine all that free bandwidth on the humanity router.

- Get out of bed and take a seat in meditation.
- Close your eyes and follow your Easy Breath for a few moments.
- Consider all the people asleep.
- The plants asleep.
- The sky asleep.
- The earth asleep.
- The waters of the world asleep.
- Imagine the night sky as a beautiful, dark, velvet blanket that wraps around you, keeping you comforted and calm.
- Sense the beating of your heart, a quiet drumming in the night. The quietness of your breath ...
- On your next out-breath begin to let out a little humming sound, let it be slow and easy.
- Continue humming on your out-breath for ten breaths.
- When you are finished, take yourself back off to bed feeling magical and ready for sweet dreams.

DAYS OFF

Hoorah ... it's your day off! Twenty-four hours of fun tokens yet to be spent. Here we can share some mindful ways to while away your leisure days, from enhancing your creativity to getting fit.

UPON RISING: give yourself a little longer to meditate today and see what happens. Try the Just Being Meditation on page 91 and follow this with some gentle stretching.

JOURNAL: make a luxury hot drink. In your journal, reflect on three things you might be grateful for today.

BRUNCH: time to freshen up. Exercise, especially if chosen with fun in mind, can become a beautiful meditation on movement and energy.

DE-CLUTTER: clean your living space with love, tidying away clutter and keeping hold of the things that bring you joy.

AFTERNOON: head out to a museum or gallery and meditate on the works of one of your favourite artists.

CONNECT WITH NATURE: take a walk outside and appreciate the beauty of a flower. No matter how many thoughts we might be having, nature is always there, quietly fulfilling itself.

FALL IN LOVE: recite love poetry. Swap the romantic interest of the piece (usually a him or a her) for something a little larger and dedicate the recital to life itself. When we smile at life, life often smiles back.

AT THE CLOSE OF DAY: sound your way into a new day, setting fresh intentions and getting a great night's sleep.

TIP: A relaxed schedule gives life extra room to be spontaneous with you. Set off into your day with an air of openness and an attitude of 'I wonder what will happen today?'

FITNESS

Why not start the day by breaking out in a sweat? When you are in the mood, there is nothing quite like a morning workout. Especially if the whole affair canters nicely towards a cafe crescendo with some of your favourite wellness friends.

Still not keen? Here are some ideas to get you going ...

1. Find a form of exercise you enjoy. If you don't enjoy it, perhaps find something that you at least find pleasant as means of keeping you fit, agile and well.

2. Oftentimes the aversion we feel arises at the mere thought of doing something. That's the key bit to notice, the negative thoughts. Once we actually get started It's usually not so bad after all – and often quite enjoyable if we are well engaged.

3. Ask yourself, 'What's the intention here?' Exercising for the joy of movement and the feeling of doing good to your body brings its own motivation.

4. Be present: when you're interested in your movement you'll come to learn lots about your body. You might also discover many new and interesting forms of exercise.

Housework

As well as formal workouts where our physical activity is called exercise, there are many other chances to be active on our free days. Take, for example, housework – a great way to burn calories, reorganise your life and clear away clutter.

Someone once told me that a house represents the body in dreams. I don't know if this is always true for me, but my state of consciousness and the kitchen floor often do share something of a common condition ...

Meditation: Everything Is Special

(30 minutes, plus)

- As you clean your home, imagine that everything you encounter is an externalisation of yourself.
- With this in mind, treat everything you touch with reverence.
- Some people like to imagine that everything they encounter around the house is a part of themselves, whereas others prefer a more material analogy; for example, treating everything as though it were fashioned from a rare and precious gem!
- Whichever approach you settle on, try to keep this focus for the duration of the housework, and perhaps extend throughout the day as part of a longer exploration.

ART AND BEAUTY

A relaxed day-off often creates the perfect window for enjoying the beautiful things in life; an open invitation to let go of the regular world's hand and wander freely.

For you, that might entail a visit to your local art gallery or exhibition centre. You might like to try your hand at something creative too, such as dancing, entrepreneurship or even flower arranging.

Sometimes simply being outside among the elements offers more beauty than we could shake a stick at. The appreciation of natural beauty and of art is a great form of meditation. Just like conventional practices, beautiful things offer us an express ride to The Middle.

For example, we might spot a beautiful painting, bird or sunrise; then and there, we experience a brief moment of peace. Time stops and we are stilled – entirely in awe and positively lost in beauty.

Wow.

On that note – let's go to the gallery!

Meditation: Connecting with a Work of Art

(15 minutes)

Stand at a comfortable viewing distance from your desired piece and take a few Easy Breaths.

Let your eyes gaze loosely on the piece, not reaching in or searching or picking it apart. Not opining, just being there with the work of art.

In the same way as you undressed the banana in Part Three of this book, see the *beingness* of this piece.

Let it unfold itself in you, let it take you along.

When you are ready, return your attention to your surroundings in the present moment.

Meditation: Stepping into a Painting

(5 to 10 minutes)

Again, stand a comfortable viewing distance away from your chosen painting. Take a few Easy Breaths.

In your imagination, step into the picture the way you might step through a door frame.

Imagine, for example, swinging from the stars, running up the hills, kissing the beautiful maiden sitting in the carriage. Play in the painting.

If the painting has several elements or people, take turns in becoming each of them, and then explore the scene as them.

When you have explored enough, bring your attention back to the present moment.

Coffee and Pastries

Some days – during weekends, say, and high days and holidays – it's good to break with routine and indulge yourself a little. As the saying goes, 'a little of what you fancy' and all that ...

You'll need:

*   one of your favourite pastries,
*   a hot cup of organic tea, coffee or espresso.

Hold the warm cup in your hands and smell those inimitable pastry perfumes while watching the world go by.

If you happen to have a moment like this, why not reflect on how fortunate it is to be in this position, croissant in hand. At simple moments like these, life is good.

TIP: The poem 'Otherwise' by Jane Kenyon is the perfect accompaniment to moments like these.

Nurturing Your Own Creativity

The way in which your creativity expresses itself will be uniquely suited to you and the moment, so try not to be bound up in any ideas that creativity must mean a particular activity such as painting. For you, it could be origami, topiary, pimping up your wardrobe, cooking.

Some creativity is functional and arises spontaneously in response to a problem that wants solving, for instance:

1 delicious dinner needed + several odd vegetables in the fridge = creative meal solution.

You might make something out of love for someone, such as a home-cooked meal or a newly assembled bike. Or you could make something purely out of a love for life itself, with the thrill of seeing one of your visions take physical form in the world for yourself and others to share in.

When you next have a free afternoon, why not spend an hour or two exploring what creativity means to you?

Meditation: Being With a Flower

(5 minutes)

This simple meditation is a good way to open up to the beauty that's all around us.

- Choose a potted plant and place it a comfortable distance away from you.
- Take an Easy Seat, close your eyes and enjoy five Easy Breaths.
- When you feel Ready, open your eyes and explore the plant, giving it all your attention.
- Notice the way it appears to you, its shape and colour.
- Take your attention to its texture and feel. Gently touch a leaf or a petal perhaps, appreciating its intricacy.
- Move a little closer if need be and take in its fragrance. Notice the fragrance itself, but also the sensation of smelling. What is it like, to smell?
- Consider where the plant might have come from, the many stages of development it could have passed through before now, and those yet to come.
- Notice how innocent and straightforward it is. Everyone can enjoy its beauty, bees and humans alike.
- Before you bring your time with the flower to a close, sit for a moment and sense its being – in the same way we did together with the banana on page 91.
- Simply sit with it as part of life's grand tapestry, both of you unfolding moment by moment.
- Close your meditation with three conscious breaths.

TIP: Don't forget to lavish praise upon your petunias. Flowers love a bit of conversation!

Get Lost in Nature

(30 minutes)

Here's an activity worth exploring. Forest bathing, also called *shinrin-yoku*, is a Japanese stress-management activity that encourages people to enjoy their hobbies in the healing atmosphere of the forest.

We don't all have access to the forest, but we can find our nearest local green space and make some outdoors plans. Try a short walk, some fitness exercises in the garden or simply sitting on your front porch with a cup of tea.

LOVE

Leisure time is made for lovers – an occasion for meeting new people, spending time with your partner, or nursing a broken heart.

When love blossoms, it can become not only a celebration of life, but also your spiritual practice. You and your loved one help each other to grow and stay present, blowing wind in one another's sails.

Then, as the fairy dust settles, perhaps you learn something else about love. Being in love can numb all your other senses, but once the general life anaesthesia delivered by the lover comes to an end, old feelings of discontent might pop up. This is when being present and compassionate can help us navigate our way through our emotions.

Relationships can trigger our defences, reactions and plenty of finger-pointing. Through meditation we are encouraged to turn that finger right back around so that we might discover if the source of the rattling is located inside us rather than out there.

A mindfulness practice can help us in those times where we might need to be forgiving or understanding. Both to ourselves and our loved one. It's not always easy and we don't always get it right.

TIP: Read the novel *Love in the Time of Cholera* by Gabriel García Márquez or the poem 'The Mule Got Drunk and Lost in Heaven' by Hafiz.

With A New Love

Wow wee. Ding dong! You're all butterflies and sparkling gin fizz. Just think of all the wonderfulness this union will enable you to share and give! (And who here doesn't appreciate a generous lover?)

Being in love shows a person who they really are. The first throes of love relieve you of all and any prior worries. You waltz around the office, the roses smell sweeter and life's a box of organic veg.

If that weren't enough, many other synchronous events begin to show up in your life, seemingly reflecting the glow in your heart. Oh, how beautiful it is to fall in love ...

This part of love is the clearest intimation of our true nature. It just took our lover to help reveal it.

But here's a thought: it's not the lover we love, but love itself.

Nine Poems to Fall in Love With

(... and a short story about love triangles)

Nine Poems

- 'I Would Live in Your Love' and 'It Is Enough for Me' by Sara Teasdale.
- 'Take For Example This' and 'I Like My Body When It is with Your Body' by e. e. cummings.
- 'The Passionate Shepherd to His Love' by Christopher Marlowe.
- 'The Story of Love' by Kabir.
- 'Love in the Bathtub' by Sujata Bhatt.
- 'Listening' by D. H. Lawrence.
- 'As I Walked Out One Evening' by W. H. Auden.

A Short Story

'Schools and Schools' by O. Henry.

Meditation: Heartbreak

(15 minutes)

Heartbreak can be so terribly painful. It often comes as an unexpected reminder that nothing is safe and things rarely stay the same. The topic of relationships is such a huge one that a thorough discussion of it surpasses the scope of this small book. But don't worry, here is a two-step process I've found which can act as a great springboard into Mindful Love.

Step One: Focus Your Mind

Set a timer for five minutes as you simultaneously set yourself the adventure of keeping your attention tied to your breathing for five minutes each day. Focussing the attention can help you to keep it real if your mind is running away with wild storylines and obsessive thinking of *what could have been* or *should have been*.

Step Two: Feel Your Feelings

With your mind somewhat calmer after five minutes' focusing on your breath, don't be afraid to feel your bodily feelings. Dig deep and see if you can find the beauty in this life experience you've gained. Life has many colours. Being present isn't about moving towards a life of just one shade. It is about staying receptive and welcoming the rainbow of experience. Let the raw sensations you may feel (tension, heaviness … pain, perhaps) unfold and find their place. They will soon dissolve, all things do, so give them your loving attention and see what happens. Hey, you can't really rush these things so go gently, my friend.

Book Cure

The end of love, we are advised by poet Sophie Hannah, should require the hiring of a hall in which to celebrate. What a beautiful thing it is.

Read 'The End of Love' by Sophie Hannah or 'Talking to Grief' by Denise Levertov.

A Hot Date ... With my Friend

So now you're on your own again, single and apparently destined to be alone for eternity ... But think of all that free time you now have for fostering friendships and creativity, personal enquiry and your own endeavours.

Can you be happy regardless of your romantic life – happy to just be you? This way, your happiness doesn't depend on anything else or the presence of anyone in particular. With this brimming, 'my cup floweth over' attitude, it wouldn't be a surprise if you were suddenly to find your dance card was full anyway.

And stay open-minded: many of us keep long lists about the qualities that our ideal lover should possess, but love is its own creature.

You might find love where you least expect it.

TIP: Read the short story 'Gift for a Sweetheart' by Isabel Allende and consider how you can be a great giver of love today.

Meditation: Shared Love

(10 minutes)

This is a simple meditation that you can practise whether you are in a relationship or not, as it's all about connecting with the love that's out there.

- Take an Easy Seat.
- Take some Easy Breaths for a few minutes.
- Take your attention to the area around your heart and cultivate the feeling of love. (If you need a little help feeling the love, try bringing to mind someone you love a lot – family, friends pets, cars?)
- Imagine this feeling of love as a glowing ball of light in the heart .... It grows and grows with every breath ... until it outgrows your body and spreads into the room where you're sitting.
- Imagine this love growing so large that it encompasses the whole house, town and maybe even the world.

TIP: Read Homer's *Iliad* and explore the whole spectrum of human emotion.

Meditation: Sunday Blues

(5 minutes)

So how can you learn to fall in love with the new week ahead?

We tend to give things labels (see the Undressed Banana Meditation in Part Three) in order to categorise and make sense of them. From an experiential perspective, labelling has a somewhat nullifying or de-potentiating effect. Once something has been labelled, the thing itself isn't experienced as it really is in its enormity; instead, it is conceptualised and becomes slightly less real or vivid.

If you find yourself beset by unreasonable thoughts from time to time, labelling them might reduce their impact. Here's how to get started:

- If you find yourself down in the dumps, suffering from a severe case of the Sunday blues, sit quietly and examine your thoughts.
- When a problematic or recurring thought pattern emerges, you might say: 'Oh yes, that is another guilt thought,' or 'Oh yes that's just another fear thought.'
- And know that it isn't real unless you make it so.

Meditation : Opening To A Wonderful Day Ahead

(6 minutes)

This can be a fun meditation to do as you prepare yourself for the working days that lie ahead, so do go gently with it and enjoy yourself as you chant your way into a really wonderful week.

- Sit quietly in your Easy Seat.
- Close your eyes and take some relaxing Easy Breaths.
- Keep your back nice and straight so you have the full use of your lungs.
- On your next out-breath, sound the mantra 'Aum' (or 'Om'). If you break the mantra down, it will sound a little like this: *ah–ooh–mmm*.
- You can make this sound by having your mouth make the shape of a wide-open '*ah*' sound. Then, as you are continuing the sound while breathing out, move the mouth into an almond shape to make the '*ooh*' sound, before closing the mouth finally for an '*mmm*' sound.
- Doing this in the mirror can help if you aren't sure what shape your mouth is in.
- As you breathe out, sound this Aum mantra all in one go, trying to keep the sound very equal so that each phase of the sound takes the same amount of time.
- Sound this mantra on each out-breath for about fifteen breaths, being careful not to over-breathe or strain.
- Close with a few Easy Breaths and a minute or so to sit in The Middle quietly observing all and any changes that seem to have happened in the body as a result of your little bit of Aum'ing.

TIP: Pick a positive intention for the week ahead, for example 'I live my days with strength, openness and love', and keep it in mind as you sound the mantra.

CONCLUSION

There is no conclusion – for there to be a conclusion, this would have to be the end and it's not over till the fat lady sings!

This book is all about an adventure of ongoing discovery, where you can take what you've uncovered and continue with your explorations into the art of living. Remember to revisit the meditations in this guide again and again to see if the things you find change during your practice.

BEGIN AGAIN: if you find yourself slipping into unhealthy patterns and discontent, you can pick up where you left off at any time. Meditation is not at all precious; it's always happily waiting for you, always ready to invite you in. Start with an Easy Breath. Close your eyes and you are back ...

BEGIN AFRESH: your meditation will likely change over time; different things will happen during it and the areas you are interested in will change too. This is natural, so you don't have to be hard on yourself or expect things to be a certain way.

KEEPING YOUR PRACTICE GOING: you might find that regular meditation practice keeps your garden from becoming overgrown – assuaging feelings of fear, stress and otherwise getting lost in the world.

How to Create a Daily Practice

Research suggests that mindfulness training brings a great deal of positive change to the structure of the brain. However, some of those changes do not persist in the absence of regular mindfulness meditation, so it's a good idea to create your own daily practice.

Set aside fifteen minutes a day for your meditation-related activities: put it in the diary. If you feel like you've only got a few minutes of formal meditation in you, be open to using the rest of the time for one of the other meditations in this guide, such as walking in nature or cooking a meal with presence.

Make a meditation friend so that you can encourage each another, or join a local group of like-minded people.

Keep a space at home, complete with a pillow and a comfy outfit at the ready, so that it feels more circumstantially convenient to meditate each day.

Keep your practice open, without too many expectations: it's ok if you miss a day or if your meditations don't seem to be doing anything. A bit like being bitten by the love bug, wonderful things are often whirring away at an unseen level just waiting to surprise you pleasantly.

Don't try to do too much or force it. Yes, the benefits of meditation are clear and, yes, you may remember how good it feels when you do it. Yes, it can also require a little discipline. That said, sitting there struggling, or driving yourself mad trying to meditate for ten whole, eternal minutes, is probably not helpful.

One should never, so I'm told, become a slave to one's programme. If, for instance, you have time off of an evening and you think you really should meditate ... but what you really want to do is play your guitar, then do that instead. That joy – that happiness that comes from the guitar – is a lovely meditation of itself.

But do be sure to do some meditation all the same; just like exercise, it only works if you do it!

Spontaneous Meditation

After a period of formal practice, you may find that presence of mind or feeling in the moment begin to happen spontaneously during your everyday activities. For example, you're midway through making a coffee when you realise you're on autopilot and not paying attention at all. In that instant you are aware of yourself again and you can choose to proceed with attention and care.

Every so often, the urge to meditate will solicit you. Oh yes it will! You'll just be going about your day and all of a sudden you'll feel this bubbling desire to go and sit quietly. These invitations from meditation are pure magic. Like getting a telegram from the Queen. I have found these to be some of the best times to meditate, so cherish those moments.

TIP: Read the poem 'Pax' by D. H. Lawrence.

Good Luck on Your Journey!

As the saying goes, before enlightenment drink red, carry Prada; after enlightenment, drink red, carry Prada.

If you enjoyed fashion, art, sport or red wine before learning how to practise twenty-four-hour mindfulness, then you may well still appreciate these things after. It is not the things we do that are deemed spiritual or mindful, but the attitude we take to them.

There are certain things that point us more readily to happiness, peace and beauty – and in time we find in ourselves a natural, spontaneous urge towards them. There's no pre-judgement about the things you'll be saying hello to or waving goodbye on your way ahead. There are no rules of thumb, you see. Sometimes people think that once you become mindful you have to start wearing bamboo socks, stop drinking wine and start using that eco-friendly washing powder. But, you know, it's just not true.

For sure, as you become increasingly sensitive to life you also get a deepening sense of being at one with everything else. You sense that you share something of a common ground with all other beings. When this is apparent, you may well find yourself moving towards a diet that is kind to the animals, or a home-laundry system that doesn't pollute the environment, or a clothing arrangement that feels good.

Or maybe not . . .

None of the practices in this book are the path to presence in and of themselves. We must remain willing and open-minded enough to explore each mindful activity that takes our interest on this path – because we never know what they will bring. Far better to keep our options open!

With this is mind, follow your own interests and enthusiasms, because these usually have a good route figured out for you. You can make all kinds of trips, have experiences, take jobs and meet exciting people out there in the word, but remember you have infinite worlds within you to explore. Blogs and workshops alike can't take the place of loving, candid self-exploration. Where's your inner Taj Mahal? Your personal Paris?

One thing I can tell you: if you follow the practices in these pages, slowly but surely your interest in material life will arise more and more out of joy, love and celebration. You will become more *you*, with fewer preconceptions about what form that should take or how your personality will unfold. If you are typically quite stiff upper lip, perhaps it will change, but maybe not.

This is freedom.

The freedom to be you.

TIP: Read 'Ithaka' by C. P. Cavafy.

FURTHER READING

Part One

Armitage, Simon, 'It Ain't What You Do, It's What It Does To You' in *Selected Poems of Simon Armitage* (Faber and Faber, 2001).

Bennet, Arnold, *How To Live On Twenty-Four Hours A Day* (A Word To The Wise, 2013).

Brabazon, Francis, 'Victoria Market' in *The New Oxford Book of Australian Verse*, ed. Les A. Murray (Oxford University Press, 1968).

Chekhov, Anton, *Gooseberries*, trans. Ronald Wilks (Penguin UK, 2015).

Frost, Robert, 'The Road Not Taken' in *101 Poems That Could Save Your Life*, ed. Daisy Goodwin (Harper Collins, 2003).

Gurdjieff, G.I., *Life Is Real Only Then, When I Am* (Penguin Books, 1991).

Hafiz, 'Wow' In *The Gift: Poems By Hafiz The Great Sufi Master*, trans. Daniel Ladinksy (Penguin Books, 1999).

Kennelly, Brendan, 'Begin' in *Soul Food* (Bloodaxe, 2007).

Larkin, Philip, 'Days' in *101 Poems to Get You through the Day (and night)*, ed. Daisy Goodwin (Harper Collins, 2003).

MacNeice, Louis, 'Apple Blossom' in *101 Poems That Could Save Your Life*, ed. Daisy Goodwin (Harper Collins, 2003).

Monro, Harold, 'Living' in *The Earth For Sale* (Chatto & Windus, 1928).

Part Two

Bates, H. E., *The Grapes Of Paradise* (Penguin Books, 1974).

Bloom, William, *The Endorphin Effect* (Piatkus, reprint edition, 2011).

Chekhov, Anton, 'A Misfortune' in *The Essential Tales of Chekhov*, ed. Richard Ford, trans. Constance Garnett (Granta Books, 1999)

Foster, J. quoted at http://www.audensociety.org/vivianfoster.html

Groome, David, *An Introduction to Cognitive Psychology: Processes and Disorders* (Psychology Press, 2nd edition, 2006).

Guest, Edgar Albert, 'It Couldn't Be Done' in *A Path To Home (HardPress, 2008)*

Hafiz, 'The Vintage Man' in *The Gift: Poems by Hafiz the Great Sufi Master*, trans. Daniel Ladinsky (Penguin Books, 1999).

Hafiz, 'Jumping For Joy' in *I Heard God Laughing: Poems of Hope and Joy*, trans. Daniel Ladinsky (Penguin Books, 2006).

Holub, Miroslav, 'The Door' in *Poems Before and After*, Collected English Translations (Bloodaxe Books, 2006).

Inzlicht, M. and T. Rimma, Meditation, mindfulness and executive control: the importance of emotional acceptance and brain-based performance monitoring, *Social Cognitive and Affective Neuroscience 8* (2013): 85–92.

Lessing, Doris, 'Flight' in *African Stories* (Simon & Schuster, 2014).

Levy, D., J. Wobbrock, A. Kaszniak, and M. Ostergren, The effects of mindfulness meditation training on multitasking in a high-stress information environment, *Proceedings of Graphics Interface Conference 2012* (Canadian Information Processing Society, 2012): 45–52.

Krompinger, J. and M. J. Baime, Mindfulness training modifies subsystems of attention, *Cognitive, Affective, & Behavioral Neuroscience 7* (2) (2007): 109–19.

MacNeice, Louis, 'Snow' in *Collected Poems* (Faber and Faber, 1988).

Montaigne, Michel Eyquem de, *Essays* (Penguin Classics, 1993).

Rilke, Rainer Maria, *Ahead of All Parting: The Selected Poetry and Prose of Rainer Maria Rilke* (Modern Library, 1995).

Spira, Rupert, *The Transparency Of Things* (Non-Duality Press, 2008).

Tucci, Nicolo, 'The Evolution of Knowledge' in *Tales from The New Yorker* (The New Yorker, 1947).

van Vugt, M. K. and A. P. Jha, Investigating the impact of mindfulness meditation training on working memory, *Cognitive, Affective, and Behavioral Neuroscience 11* (3) (2011):44–54.

Wells, H. G., *The New Machiavelli* (Penguin Classics, 2005).

Zeidan *et al*, Neural correlates of mindfulness meditation-related anxiety relief, *Cognitive, Affective, and Behavioral Neuroscience 7* (2) (2007): pp.109–19.

Part Three

Baudrillard, Jean, *The Ecstasy Of Communication* (MIT Press, 2012).

Conner, Cheryl, 'Wasting Time at Work: The Epidemic Continues', *Forbes Europe Online*, 31 July 2015. Retrieved 27 Sept. 2016 from www.forbes.com/sites/cherylsnappconner/2015/07/31/wasting-time-at-work-the-epidemic-continues/#32f41db3ac16

de la Mare, W., 'The Listeners' in *The Listeners and Other Poems* (ValdeBooks, 2010).

Frost, Robert, 'A Time To Talk' in *Robert Frost Poems* (St Martin's Press, 2002).

Hafiz, 'I Know the Way You Can Get' in *The Gift: Poems by Hafiz the Great Sufi Master*, trans. Daniel Ladinsky (Penguin Books, 1999).

Kallistratos, M., Midday naps associated with reduced blood pressure and fewer medications, European Society of Cardiology, *ScienceDaily* (2015). Retrieved 27 Sept. 2016 from www.sciencedaily.com/releases/2015/08/150829123659.htm

Klein, J., *I Am* (Non-Duality Press, 2016).

Lucille, F., *Eternity Now* (Non-Duality Press, 2008).

Macmillan, Angela (ed.), *A Little Aloud: An Anthology Of Prose And Poetry For Reading Aloud To Someone You Care For* (Chatto & Windus, 2010).

Reid, Erin, How people navigate expected and experienced professional identities, *Organization Science* (2015): 99–1017.

Van der Helm, E., N. Gujar and M. P. Walker, Sleep deprivation impairs the accurate recognition of human emotions, *SLEEP 33* (3) (2010): 335-342.

Part Four

Allende, Isabel, 'Gift For A Sweetheart' in *The Stories of Eva Luna* (Atria Books, 2015).

Auden, W. H., 'As I Walked Out One Evening' in *Poems (Poet to Poet)* (Faber & Faber, 2005).

Bhatt, Sujata, 'Love in A Bathtub' in *Monkey Shadows* (Carcanet Press, 1991).

Castano, E. and D. Comer Kidd, Reading literary fiction improves theory of mind, *Science 342* (6156) (2013): 377–380.

cummings, e. e., 'I like my body when it's with your body' and 'Take for example this' in *Tulips and Chimneys* (Liveright, 1997).

Dick, Philip. K ., *Minority Report* (Citadel Press, reprint edition, 2002).

Dickinson, Emily, 'I'm nobody who are you' in *I'm Nobody! Who are You? Poems of Emily Dickinson for Children* (Stemmer House Publishers, 1978).

Hafiz, 'The Mule That Got Drunk and Lost In Heaven' in *The Gift: Poems by Hafiz the Great Sufi Master*, trans. Daniel Ladinsky (Penguin Books, 1999).

Hannah, Sophie, 'The End of Love' in *Selected Poems of Sophie Hannah* (Penguin Books, 2013).

Henry, O., *Best Short Stories of O. Henry* (Random House, 1997).

Henry, O., 'Schools and Schools' in *Options* (1stworld Library, 2007).

Homer, *The Iliad*, ed. Peter Jones and trans. E. V. Rieu (Penguin Classics, 2003).

Kabir, 'The Story of Love' in *The Maxims of Kabir*, ed. G. N. Das (Abhinav Publications, 1999).

Kenyon, Jane, 'Otherwise' in *Soul Food* (Bloodaxe, 2007).

Lawrence, D. H., 'Listening' in *The Complete Poems of D. H. Lawrence* (Wordsworth Poetry Library, 1994).

Lessing, Doris, *Stories* (Everyman, 2008).

Levertov, Denise, 'Talking To Grief' in *Soul Food*, ed. Neil Astley (Bloodaxe Books, 2007).

Marlowe, Christopher, 'The Passionate Shepherd to His Love' in *Christopher Marlowe: Complete Poems and Translations* (Penguin Classic, 2007).

Márquez, Gabriel García, *Love in the Time of Cholera* (Penguin Essentials, 2016).

Maharashi, Ramana, *The Collected Works Of Ramana Maharashi* (Sophia Perennis, 2006).

McDaniel, Brandon T. and Sarah M. Coyne, The interference of technology in couple relationships and implications for women's personal and relational well-being, *Psychology of Popular Media Culture*, 5 (1) (2016): 85–98.

Teasdale, Sara, 'Live in Your Love' and 'Enough' in *The Collected Poems of Sara Teasdale*, (digireads.com, 2012).

Wells, H. G., *The Country of the Blind and Other Selected Stories* (Penguin Classics, 2007).

Conclusion

Cavafy, C. P., 'Ithaka' in *The Collected Poems with parallel Greek text* (Oxford World's Classics, 2008). Cavafy's poem '*Che Fece ... Il Gran Refiuto*' also appears in this collection – another beauty!

Lawrence, D. H., 'Pax' in *The Complete Poems of D. H. Lawrence* (Wordsworth Poetry Library, 1994).

Pessoa, Fernado, 'The Keeper of Sheep' in *A Little Larger Than the Entire Universe: Selected Poems* (Penguin Classics, 2006).

ACKNOWLEDGEMENTS

A thousand appreciations go to Laura Horsley for her kindness and talent in editing this book, taking it enthusiastically through its every evolution. Thank you to Sue Lascelles for her brilliant advice and generosity in working on the manuscript.

I would like to thank all of my teachers, with a special thank you to Carole Leonard-Morgan.

My appreciation also goes to Adam: thank you for encouraging me to write this book and for offering the buoyancy, time and space to complete it. My gratitude goes also to my family for their love, and all the many new friends I have met through this work who have shared in this grand exploration with me.

MEDITATION INDEX